Composing Ourselves:

Writing from the Composition Program at Missouri State University

Composing Ourselves:

Writing from the Composition Program at Missouri State University

Second Edition

Edited by Lori Feyh and Ken Gillam
Missouri State University

Springfield, Missouri
2009

For inquiries contact
Editor, *Composing Ourselves: Writing from the Composition Program at Missouri State University*
Missouri State University
English Department
901 South National Avenue
Springfield, MO 65897

Cover photograph and design: Ken Gillam

Library of Congress Cataloging in Publication Data

Composing ourselves : writing from the composition program at Missouri State University / edited by Lori Feyh and Ken Gillam.
   2nd ed.
   p. cm.
 ISBN 978 0 913785 16 4
1. College prose, American Missouri Springfield. 2. Teachers' writings, American Missouri Springfield. 3. American essays 21st century. 4. Academic writing. 5. College readers. 6. Missouri State University. I. Feyh, Lori. II. Gillam, Ken.
 PS683.C6C67 2009
 808'.0427 dc22

                      2009027773

Editorial Team

Lori Feyh   Editor

Ken Gillam   Editor

Kevin Luebbering   Managing Editor

Angelia Northrip Rivera   Production Editor

Holly Corbett   Associate Editor

Diana Tucker   Associate Editor

Table of Contents

Chapter Three: Rhetorical Analyses

Chapter Four: Textual Responses

Appendix

Introduction

Lori Feyh

THIS SECOND EDITION of *Composing Ourselves: Writing from the Composition Program at Missouri State University* reflects the commitment of our program, as well as the Missouri State University English department, to engage students in the art of making meaning. Members of our department and students active in our courses view writing as just that: a way of making meaning; a way of knowing—both the self and the world. Such attempts at making and communicating meaning are found here in the essays submitted by students enrolled in various levels of composition courses, as well as essays submitted by their "teachers": both graduate students and professors who write alongside their students, becoming neither a student nor a teacher, but merely a peer.

Our collection begins with a series of non sourced essays, loosely defined by the genre of memoir, which encourages writers to reflect upon what is found in the world around us and struggle through writing to discover that which is already within us. This is writing from a first person perspective that is rooted in reflection and analysis, and it reminds all of us that before we begin searching for the experts outside ourselves—those experts found behind podiums and inside hard bound volumes—we must look for the experts that reside within.

Of course, there are those to whom we must also turn for expertise, and our attempts at connecting the experts outside with the experts within can be found in the source based essays contained in the second half of our collection. Learning to accommodate sources in our writing is more than merely developing our knowledge of citation and documentation, it is truly an exercise in academic conversation. When using sources to illustrate a point or claim evidence for argument, students are also engaging in a paper bound conversation that exists between professionals in the academic community—a community that has previously been outside the realm of our students. To enter such conversation, students must attempt the delicate balance of maintaining a critical distance from scholarly sources, enabling them to analyze and evaluate the arguments of so called experts, while at the same time present themselves as legitimate partners in academic conversation by adopting the language use of scholars, through word choice, syntax, textual design, and documentation.

All of the works collected here, both sourced and non sourced, began where all texts begin: with a writer facing a blank page or screen confronting a plethora of voices both from within and without. This dilemma is faced by members of our classrooms, including the students featured within, through the aid of the writing process. Viewing writing as a process existing of manageable steps that lead a writer to articulate in an effective manner what had previously been jumbled thoughts and voices allows us to see writing for what it is: a craft rather than an art—a craft that creates a continuous conversation between readers and writers and the ongoing conversations in the world. The writers featured here have offered their side of the conversation; now, it is up to you, as readers, to respond. You are welcome to enter.

Chapter One:

Unsourced Writing

Welcome to South Dakota

Jane Hoogestraat

SIMON AND GARFUNKEL'S "HOMEWARD BOUND" is playing on the tape deck. It is after midnight and I have just gotten into a car with three strangers at the Sioux Falls airport. We are fifty miles from Brookings on I–29. I speak quietly with the driver. The other two passengers speak more quickly to one another in Tamil. All three are electrical engineers from India, studying at SDSU, where my father taught for many years. Fifteen miles out, I turn to the woman from Madras who has never been on this straight black road before, never seen such open space, and say, "Those are the lights of Brookings. You won't be able to see them again for awhile, but they are there. I grew up on this road."

Shortly before 2 A.M., I will ask to be dropped off near Brookings High School. I want to walk, I say, the few blocks to my family's place, to clear my head. The streets are completely silent, the air, even in early August, is sharp and clear. In the entryway of my parent's condo, I hesitate, then ring the buzzer once. I am immediately admitted, and say only: "I have a story."

The story started at 3:00 the afternoon before in Chicago's O'Hare. I have spent days of my life here, and want to see the long glass walkway again. I glance to the left, see a green sky and think, "That's odd. That looks like a pop up storm. Chicago doesn't have those." Twenty minutes later, all ground and air traffic has stopped. Planes on the ground waiting to be unloaded are parked because the lightning makes it unsafe for anyone to be outside.

Back in the gate area, the flight to Syracuse is delayed because the plane from Sioux Falls is not on the ground yet. I have dealt with this before. I know that I will have plenty of time to find a Starbucks stand, a *New York Times*, and a book on *How to be a Great Boss* that I would not be seen with anywhere else. Ever. In a seat next to me, I notice a young woman with skin darker than mine, although not by much, flipping through the pages of her passport. In another seat close, someone clearly dressed for Syracuse. None of this is unusual. I have one foot in the generation that still dressed up for flights. Blazer, hose, matching purse and case, jewelry from my friend Carolyn that matches my blazer, neck pillow. It is not unusual for other women traveling alone to sit next to me. I look (and am) safe, and they can sense it.

She started in Madras thirty hours ago, transferred through Frankfurt, cleared customs in Chicago. She thinks she is two hours away from landing in South Dakota. She will be studying at SDSU in the masters program to be an electrical engineer. She has never been stateside before. The language of instruction in Madras is English. I tell her not to worry about the delay to Syracuse—it isn't our plane. I tell her that I am not an expert, but that I always went to school far away from home. The woman who is actually flying to Syracuse, almost certainly another academic, listens politely, smiles, and then drifts away. Before long, the flight to Syracuse is canceled.

When the flight to Sioux Falls is canceled, I tell the agent at the gate: "We didn't start together, but we are traveling together now." He books us both standby on the next flight (already delayed), my ticket more quickly because it is electronic. Looking at her paper ticket, he says "The only thing I can tell you is don't lose that ticket." I offer the use of my cell phone. Every hour or so, she calls her friends in Brookings, or they call her. She sleeps, not enough. She cries a little, and I can say nothing to help.

A rumor moves through the gate area that the standby list goes by the number of frequent flyer miles. I know that means I will be on the flight, and she will not. I don't tell her that. I do explain that we can't take a cab for the 600 miles from Chicago to our town on the northern high plains. I know that it is time to buy another neck pillow, another water bottle, and something to eat. I ask if she has any dietary restrictions. She is a vegetarian. I prepare to spend the night in O'Hare.

After 10:30, when the flight is finally boarding, the first name called on the standby list is mine. I put my hand on her shoulder and say, "Not yet." In front of us, a very angry young woman and a very drunk young man are complaining about how long they have been waiting. The process stops for ten minutes before the list of names resumes. She says, "Don't leave me" and then "Pray for me." When the last name has been called, I am still standing near the door with a boarding pass and a matching blazer. There are still seats available, but the crew has run out of time for boarding. Suddenly, an agent notices me and says, "Wait a minute, did she volunteer?" Politely and quietly I say, "I am not getting on the plane without her." I look around at two gate agents who have worked too long, and three yellow slickered runway workers who have been out all day in the rain. Together, the agents decide to print the last boarding pass of the day. And suddenly, we are all smiling. We will be home late, but we will be home.

There is quiet applause on the plane, one or two people (who have been following the story and wishing her well) say "Welcome to South Dakota." When we are in the air, I deliver her water bottle back and say, "Yes, I did reach your friends. They will be meeting us."

Sojourn Home: Knocked Up, Not Knocked Out

Lerner Kolb

STANDING IN JIM'S BATHROOM in Toledo, the cold, hard, salmon/terracotta Spanish ceramic tiles were pressing up on my bare feet as the two pink lines of a similar color appeared on the pregnancy test instead of one. I thought to myself, "Okay. Okay. Okay. Okay. Okay. Everything is going to be OKAY." I took a couple of deep breaths in through my nose and out through my mouth, and I reached for the cold brass doorknob. It felt like a hundred pounds of resistance turning in my hand before it gave way and pulled in toward me so I could start walking down the stairs toward the living room where Jim was waiting for the results.

He looked like something close to a train wreck when he saw the stick; he seemed like he had been run over by a semi truck and stayed that way for about three days. I could smell the red sauce bubbling on the stove for dinner, and the weight of it in my nose turned my stomach. In reality, we barely knew each other. I had only been in Toledo for about eight months; I had moved there for business. I operated half of a dozen clubs, all of which were cycled out so that we never owned any of them for more than a year or two; except for Titanium in Toledo; that was our cash cow. My job was to move around every six months or so and scout the new property. I would then buy the location, gut the inside, supervise the build out, finish up the licensing, hire the staff, train the permanent management, and pass it on to them once things were running smoothly; my specialty was the bar and wait staff. We would flip 'em once they profited a million a year. That's real estate jargon for "buy them cheap, fix them up, and sell them at a profit." Frank was my partner, and he provided the money and the business experience; I did the leg work and made sure everything happened the way it was suppose to. Have you ever seen *Roadhouse?* I was kind of like Patrick Swayze.

We had taken on a two fer project by hanging onto Titanium in Toledo while starting a new place called The Kiss in Detroit. Since the two were only about forty five minutes apart it was fairly easy to manage them simultaneously. I was working about 120 hours a week and felt like walking death at any given point in time. The money was insanely good, but the lifestyle had certainly taken it out of me. I was burned out and worn out, and I knew I needed a vacation. I told Francis he would have to cover for me for a week while I disappeared and got some sleep. He knew me well enough to know that if he did not take my word for it I would probably have a nervous breakdown, so I got my week.

The second day of my vacation I was sitting in a sushi bar. It was a couple of degrees cooler than comfortable, just to remind the patrons that the raw fish was properly refrigerated, and the smell of soy sauce brought the taste of it to my tongue. The bar stools were chrome with padded black saucer seats, and the half back was stick straight so that it was impossible to ever get comfortable. As a result, every one was left sitting upright as if they were in a job interview or their grandmothers were watching very closely. I noticed the music that was playing in the background sounded like something from an officer's club in the old Vietnam War movies when this bubbly, blond haired, blue eyed girl named Julie introduced herself and her friends to me. We all started talking as her boyfriend, Shawn, walked in. Long story short: Shawn and Jim were best friends, and after I knew all of Shawn's obscure records, he introduced us.

I spent the rest of my vacation being wined and dined by the older, charming, handsome mystery that was sitting across the living room from me that night with the pregnancy test in his hand. We went out on Lake Erie on his speedboat and his houseboat and we drove to Ann Arbor on his motorcycle and went camping. We felt like we had known each other forever and stayed up until dawn talking about everything that came to mind, instead of making ourselves go to sleep.

The novelty faded shortly after nature proved once again that the biological evolution of a species will always take precedence over two people trying to get their rocks off; eventually reproduction always wins. My lifestyle in general did not really scream, "Mommy!" So I gave Frank the sudden, and not so great, news. It was not much longer than a week or two after finding out that I was pregnant that I packed all of my belongings that really mattered into my brand new, champagne colored Toyota Corolla and tied my queen sized pillow top mattress to the roof of my car with blue nylon ratchet straps for the eleven hour drive home.

I stopped at a Subway for a bite to eat on the Ohio/Illinois border—the sky looked like bedlam was near, and that was the last time during my trip that I saw the sun. I drove straight into a rainstorm, or perhaps it followed right behind me, but either way I was soaked in torrential rain virtually the entire way. By the time I reached Springfield, the plastic wrap that was "protecting" my mattress had peeled back completely from the front of it and had been blown back so that one half of my mattress was a soggy sponge before I got home. Everywhere I stopped for gas someone tried to help me rewrap it, but I always graciously declined. It seemed pretty futile at that point and besides, it would dry out eventually. I was just grateful for the dose of rural hospitality. Toledo and Detroit would sooner shoot you than help you—I'll take a good ol' boy in a pickup truck any day.

I will spare you the overly involved, "Then I got fat and pregnant and went through a gruesome delivery" story. Just fast forward to February 6th, 2004; it was the day after Makaio (his name rhymes with Ohio and means, "Gift from

God," in Hawaiian) was born, and we were being released from the hospital. All I could think as I loaded him into the car was, "Okay, so I'm really taking this tiny, helpless, complex being home with me now. I have no qualifications for this, everyone's sure they don't want to stop me, right?" There it was, the resounding silence where no one protested and everyone held the peace. I was a parent. This hairy little boiled chicken was my soul responsibility, whether he liked it or not. The sentiment was echoed as we walked into the apartment, and I set his carrier down on the floor. He looked up at me for a second, and I felt the hanging pressure of an awkward silence, so I did what any reasonable person would do—I filled it with pointless conversation.

"So, this is home, for now anyway. At some point in the near future, I plan to get a yard for you to run around in. So, just hang tight. Of course, by, 'near future,' I mean in relation to all of eternity, so don't hold your breath either. That crappy, respectable, hourly job I took doesn't really have, 'Lap of Luxury,' written all over it, but we'll get there." By the time the evening was over Makaio had heard about my political orientation, my spiritual beliefs, and my general moral stance in the world. He seemed to agree, as indicated by the occasional gurgle or coo, but I could tell he was strongly opposed to Hilary in '08 when he let out the biggest dirty diaper you have ever seen just at the mere mention of it.

After a year of infant care, breast feeding, diaper changes, no sleep, and some of the sweetest moments of my life, I decided that our schedule had settled to a point that I might be able to go back to school. I walked onto campus feeling like I had a huge sandwich sign, "LOOK AT THE FREAK. SHE'S NOT BEEN IN CLASS IN EIGHT YEARS, AND THERE'S PROBABLY SOME SPIT UP SOMEWHERE ON HER CLOTHING." It was a rocky start, but I fell back into stride pretty quickly and remembered that I used to be pretty good at this academic thing. Newly equipped with life skills that made time management, study skills, and motivation a cakewalk, I realized that I not only belonged here—I flourished here.

Now, Makaio is two and he amazes me daily with his stubborn, ornery, hysterical, sweet natured antics. He has taught me more about love, kindness, patience, and responsibility than twenty two other years of living combined. We have not just survived the last three years; our life is actually pretty damn good. I wake up every morning around 5:30, and I am on campus from 8:00 until 11:00. I work from 11:15 until 5:30 p.m., and then I go pick Makaio up from preschool. We go home and I make dinner, which is done just in time for his bath. Afterwards, we play and read some books until 7:30 p.m. so that he can go to bed. I usually study until my brain hurts and then I quilt. Yes, I am an honorary eighty year old and I quilt (shut up), while listening to music or watching a movie. I have taken up residence on the Dean's List, I supervise a handful of the most incredible women I have ever had the pleasure of working with, and I am more honest, trustworthy, loving, patient, and understanding than I (or anyone else) ever thought I could be. Makaio is the most incredible, stubborn, sensitive, funny little Buddha I have ever known, and I am more enriched everyday by sharing in his life.

Thank you, Monster!

—Love, Momma

A Turning Point in My Life:
My First Symphony

Rachel Hoops

IT WAS A COLD SATURDAY evening in December, and I was nine years old. Mom, Dad, and I had put on our best clothes—my parents both in black and I in a little red dress. I was going to the symphony with my parents for the first time, and I did not know what to expect. It was novel for me to be able to join my parents for an evening of entertainment, so I was happy and eager for whatever was to come.

My father parked the blue Crown Victoria and as the cold wind whipped our faces, our family of three made our way inside Juanita K. Hammons Hall for the Performing Arts. It was like a warm beacon of light. As soon as I walked into the lobby, I was enveloped by a crowd of fancily dressed, middle aged patrons. There were no other children in sight; I was the only nine year old there. In the beautiful lobby with a giant pearl chandelier, I heard the dull roar of the symphony goers' chatter. Smiles painted with bright red lipstick and the smell of perfume added to my excitement. I was glad to be a part of such an elegant group of people. I knew something exciting was about to happen, but I had no idea what.

I gave the friendly male usher my ticket and made my way up to the balcony. My parents and I sat in the front. I leaned way over the railing to get a good look at the stage below, the cold metal bar pressed against my waist. What a sight! Several musicians, all dressed in black, filled the stage. I plopped down in my cushioned, spring loaded seat and beheld the vast array of instruments. The gleam of brass caught my eye, and giant wooden basses stood out to me like elephants. I saw flutes, bassoons, timpani, trumpets, and oboes—all for the first time. My parents had played recordings of classical music since before I could walk. Never before, however, had I seen the instruments that made these glorious sounds in person.

The lights dimmed, and out walked a man with the smallest of stringed wooden instruments—the violin. The rest of the orchestra sat in attention when he walked onto the stage. I turned to my mother and asked in a loud whisper, "Who is that man?" My mother replied, "He is called the concertmaster. He helps the symphony tune." I glanced past my mother at the woman sitting next to her. She was a pinch faced, elderly woman with a permanent scowl. She put her index finger quickly to her lips as a sign for me to be quiet. Apparently, talking was not allowed.

The concertmaster put his violin beneath his chin and drew out a single pitch—an A—with his bow. After a few seconds of silence, the entire orchestra erupted in response. I was amazed at what command the concertmaster had over the orchestra, and I decided that the violin must be the most important instrument of all. When he was finished tuning, the conductor walked briskly onto the stage with her white baton.

I heard a series of C minor chords: dee dee dee dumm! I immediately recognized the first tune they played. It was Beethoven's Fifth Symphony. I became entranced with the fact that I was actually seeing musicians perform live for the first time. The strains were familiar, yet somehow hearing them in person made them come alive. The music washed over me and captivated me until the very last chord. After the piece was finished, I stood on my feet and clapped with great appreciation. The experience was almost religious.

The minutes passed quickly, and it was already time for intermission. I came back down to the lobby and got a sip of cool water from the drinking fountain. I was contemplating, all the while, how I would become a part of a symphony just like the one in the concert hall. "How do you play an instrument?"

I wondered. I wanted to be a part of the action. What could be better than creating that lovely music?

I found my parents in the crowd. We came back up the stairs to see the second half of the program. This time, the music was quite different. The piece was slow and calm. Then, a few measures in, a beautiful, haunting melody floated from the violin section to my ears. Again, I was in awe. After the refrain reiterated a few times, the concertmaster had a solo. His violin sang, and the music soared above the rest of the orchestra. It was as if the whole symphony was supporting his instrument.

I knew, at that moment, the violin was the instrument for me. I wanted to be able to produce those beautiful sounds myself. The violin seemed to be the crowning jewel of the orchestra, with its high pitched song. I knew then, without ever having touched a violin, that I wanted it to be a part of my life forever. That evening was the beginning of my life long love affair with that instrument.

The music ended, and I clapped ecstatically for the second time. I left with a thrill in my heart at the new and exciting notion that I might someday be able to play the violin myself. My parents and I bundled up in our coats once more and walked back to our car. All the way home, I bombarded Mom and Dad with questions about playing the violin. Could I play one at the age of nine? How does is work? When could I start?

Luckily at my church the next morning, my parents talked with a violinist who played in all of the morning services. Her name was Pat Lockhart. She was kind and amiable, and she answered all of our questions. As it turned out, nine was a rather late age to start playing violin. Mrs. Lockhart had started at the age of five. She said she was willing to give me lessons, and my parents graciously agreed to let me have them.

I studied violin with Mrs. Lockhart for ten years and came to college as a violin performance major. I have never questioned what I want to do for a career: music has always been my highest priority. The first live symphony concert I attended changed me forever. It is almost hard for me to believe that one night, as a young girl, I made a decision that impacted my entire life.

Before

Rosalee Avila

IT WAS THE BEGINNING OF SPRING, 1989, and I was six years old. For as far back as I could remember it had been just my mother and me. As I take a look back to those days and times so many years ago, I realize that much would change abruptly in my life within the next several years. I would acquire a stepfather and four siblings, and during the tender ages where it feels important that everything remains the same, I would pack up and move, and then move again. I had no idea that the winds of change were blowing lustily in my direction, and on this day, of all days, I surely wouldn't have cared. All was well and quiet within my world. As the 80's love song so feverishly croons it was, "Just the two of us." In general, I can say with complete honesty that there are very few days in the entirety of my past that I recall as clearly as I recall this day. I remember that the dry California heat was cooled by the sweetest, most lingering of breezes that had pushed in from off the Pacific.

My Mother and I called a small, no name apartment complex on the west side of California's capital our home. The neighborhood, I understand now, was nothing to write home about. In fact, it was downright dodgy. In those days, the fires between the two local gangs still blazed out of control, and we lived on a block where the buildings were all peeling and crumbling, the gutters overflowing with trash. The markets were all dingy, family owned operations and cars were all rusted and creepy, boat like monsters. Today, though, the breeze was lifting away the odor of the sewers and the sun was warming the grass on which I played, and to me, this day was a small piece of heaven. Our apartments were an off brown bunch of buildings that all faced inwards, so that they might look out over the same large, sprawling patch of grass.

Now, this grass was a favorite place for parents to send their children as the evening air swelled with the scents of Asian, South African, American, and Middle Eastern meals. It was also home to every would be tanner and wanna be (city style) outdoorsmen, for the neighborhood had no park, no nearby conservation area, no relaxing bike route or walking trail. Many a tenant would, on cool and hot evenings alike, pop the top off an ice cold brew or pour a bit of old time lemonade or sweet iced tea and haul out the old fold up chairs to relax and re hash with family and neighbors the events of the week.

The sun was warm upon my baby skin and the clouds were thick and plushy white balls of cotton floating in a deep sea of lapis lazuli. My mother lay outside in the sun with her honey brown curls loose about her shoulders, her thin body stretched out across the unruly grass. Deep in an Agatha Christy, she rested her head on one slender arm while the other arm held her book up in such a way that it shielded her eyes from the sun. At this age I still found no satisfaction in seeing my mother enjoying herself so thoroughly without my involvement. Quietly, I stretched my body out beside her and there I lay completely aware of her every move; the rise and fall of her ample chest; the quick, intense scanning of her eyes, from left to right, left to right, then the rustling of a turned page.

I studied her oval face, wide eyes, silky tresses, her long fingers and strong hard working hands. My mother was a lady of subtle beauty with soft golden green eyes and a warm peaches and rose's complexion. I recall with clarity the way the light played upon the tendrils of hair catching in her lashes and on her lips and I remember thinking, "How I love her!"

I must have been fiddling and wiggling in an absent minded fashion, for the next thing I knew she was waving one arm in a distracted manner.

"Oh! For goodness' sakes, Rosa, go and play."

She flipped over so abruptly that I blinked. For a moment or two I lay silent, and yet, I never could stop there. With hesitance I almost whispered, "Mom?"

Slowly—indeed painfully—she drew her book down from her face and looked at me, eyes alight with a mixture of irritation, feigned patience and love that I would later recognize as the look ordained for all children from mothers immersed in something that was not supposed to include small, whiny, needing voices.

"Rosa?" My mother made it clear she was impatiently waiting.

I was silent a moment or two. Content to bask in her attention, I lay listening to the breeze with my arms behind my head. I sighed. My mother sighed. We almost sighed together…and she closed her book and snuggled near to me. I will always remember the aroma of my real mother. Her soft lingering fragrance of Avon bubble bath, Vanderbilt's White Shoulders par' fume and clean flesh haunt me even today while strolling through the mall or mingling in settings filled with people.

"It is pretty today, isn't it?" she said, more to herself than to me.

"Yeah Mama, it is," I whispered into her hair.

I know, now, that this was the calm before the storm, a sweet memory of life before the complications that would soon be barreling through our doors. There was no way I could have known then that my mind would forever enshrine that moment within my memory. Nor could I have known, on that spring day, that many years later, this memory would be the one to inspire a life altering move across the states to reunite a mother and daughter, a move which would begin the rebuilding of a relationship between the two.

Finding My Team

Craig A. Meyer

I WAS ON A BASEBALL TEAM called the Bumblebees for several of my childhood years. We had bright yellow shirts with black letters and numbers. I loved those shirts. They gave me a sense of identity and belonging. I can remember how my teammates and I would win almost every game. The happy parents (of our team at least) always had a celebration. The party that followed was certain to have plenty of sugary fruit juices and various jiggling salads. These parties are where I learned to avoid "party" foods that had rainbow like colors and shook more than the video *Rumpshaker*. As my support system, dad was at every game. Well—okay, not exactly a support system: he came mostly because the ball fields were across the street or he had to drive me to them.

I was never a star player, just the average outfielder who got a ball hit to him every two or three innings. There were times I would daydream about some alien race or commando group I had to attack to save everybody (and I do mean everybody: I was the last person who could do it). These "missions" were actually more fun than the baseball games. I can remember once or twice even running around the outfield acting out my Earth saving story. In those times in which I was in never never land and by some miracle a ball was hit to me, the yells from teammates and parents would snap me out of my daydream. I would dutifully retrieve the ball and throw it with my wimpy little arm as far as I could (which often was between shortstop and the pitcher on my best days). After I threw the ball back, I would feel bad for not paying better attention to the game, but that was soon replaced with an attack by Klingons that I had to defend against in order to save my home world.

After several years on the Bumblebees I was "traded," which is just a fancy term to say my parents didn't sign me up fast enough to be on the team that had been mine since I started playing baseball. The Beetles was my new team, and I was about as excited about them then as I am now about my receding hairline. The first communication I had with the team's coach informed me that I needed to bring a white t shirt to our first practice. *What? Are you telling me we don't have custom printed color shirts?* Yep, no custom shirts, but plain white tees with the ever colorful black marker to write "Beetles" at a forty five degree angle across the chest. I suppose the angle was supposed to make it look cool, but it didn't. The writing on the shirt looked stupid—and cheap. After about twenty minutes of looking at this goofy shirt, I started to look at my new teammates. This team had some star players, which oddly were the coach's son and nephew, both named Mike. One of the Mikes was blond and the other had brown hair, which is how I ended up telling the two apart.

During one of our first games, I started running toward the outfield, but the coach called me back.

"You're playing catcher this game, OK?" he said.

I stared at him in confusion and then disgust. First, we did not have cool t shirts, and second, I was told to be catcher. I considered my options. None. He guided me by the shoulders to the dreaded spot behind the plate, where baseballs come directly at your crotch at the speed of sound. As he guided me, he gave me basic directions for the position: catch the ball, throw it to the pitcher, and don't let any runner get by you—ever. That was it, no inspiring or profound statements about the position or parables to make me smile. Nothing.

There I am standing behind the plate with no protective gear, looking like an idiot with my plain white and black magic markered "Beetles" t shirt and outfielder's glove. After several awkward moments of looking at my dad and at my old position in the outfield, the coach's wife ran over and dressed me in the proper gear: facemask (with helmet), chest plate (which covered my groin), and shin guards. She offered a consoling, "You'll do great!" as she trotted back to the stands. Great was the last thing on my mind.

Feeling like a little boy in a spacesuit, I knelt down and prepared to catch baseballs careening at my manhood. My mind began to wander through forests full of commandos waiting for me to eliminate them. Suddenly, a baseball walloped me in the chest plate, snapping me out of my daydream as I fell backward onto my butt. This obviously was not the place to fantasize about being Rambo. After several more throws, I began to get the hang of protecting my assets. While the baseball never got softer when I missed it, my skill compounded each week and I actually got better.

After each week's game there was no party, no celebration, and no nothing except a walk home with my dad. In the beginning, I missed the cheesy parties and dangerous food choices, but I learned that this team was different. They wanted to play baseball and go home. If I were to compare the two, my old team would be from the suburbs, and my new team would be from a trailer park. Both were good teams, just different.

Toward the end of the season with the Beetles, I actually liked the team that I once despised. We were winning games, and I was almost a star in my new position. The team depended on me each week to keep runs at bay, literally. Finally, it came down to one playoff game at Martin Luther King Jr. Park, the only game I ever played there. It was on the edge of the ghetto, but it was a clean and modernized park. This field was one of the best in the city, though my perspective of dirt never changed, so it did not matter to me. I remember that crowd being bigger than normal for our games, more family and friends. I know it was a playoff game but still it was the Beetles, not the Bumblebees. It seemed like every player had the whole family there—even my mom was there. My mom and sports is like a caveman and a computer. I was playing well, catching foul balls and striking fear into every runner who dared to round third—or at least that was my goal.

The game came down to the ninth inning and the mighty Beetles were up by one lonely run. The other team's first batter struck out after several futile swings. The next batter was their big boy—that is, he was over five foot six—as compared to the rest of us, barely five feet tall when standing on a soapbox. He swung his mighty bat and nailed the ball to centerfield. He rounded first but was halted there by our alert outfield (now that I was not out there). The next batter was a smaller boy with an Ichabod Crane type walk who had just about as much grace when swinging at nothing but air. He swung well before the ball was even near the plate, which made me laugh out loud. Finally, after two strikes he hit the ball in a unique way: he swung at the ball, missed and as he was spinning around the second time, he hit the ball! He didn't even know he had hit it when I jumped up and snatched the ball, tagging him out. Even his coach was laughing at him. The next batter arrived at the plate and had the gall to say, "Watch this."

This newest batter was about my size and build with a Louisville Slugger in his hands. Every player knows that a Slugger is the bat of champions. He tapped his cleats with the mystical bat, then readied his body to smack one beyond the fence. The first pitch he let go: it was a little outside and low. I could tell this was no ordinary moment; the crowd had hushed, and I could feel tension in the air. I cautiously tossed it back to the pitcher. The second pitch was right on the money, but he didn't bite on that one either. As I was kneeling back down after throwing the ball back, he deepened the trench beneath his right foot with his cleats, kicking dirt on my plate. GAME ON. Nobody but *nobody* kicks dirt on my plate; I shot back up ready to confront the transgressor. The umpire yelped "Time!" and showed his backside to my teammates as he swept off the plate. Order was restored.

I knelt back down and got ready to receive fastballs and curveballs. As the next pitch came, I saw the Louisville Slugger draw back and begin to swing. The bat hit the ball with a crushing blow that sent it to my old homeland of left field. The runner on first took off like a rocket. The outfield was just getting a handhold on the ball as the runner whipped around second base. The third base coach was yelling, "GO, GO, GO!" to big boy as he neared third. The outfielder heaved the baseball toward me with everything he had. The ball bounced once and I caught it—solid. With ball in mitt, I threw off my helmet and facemask. The runner had just rounded third, and his coach in the dugout screamed, "Bowl him over! Bowl him over!" I clenched my teeth.

I planted myself in front of my plate to defend it. As I tightened my grip on the ball, I could feel the stitches through the leather of my outfield glove. I looked into his eyes and he into mine, we both had an uncertainty: who was going to win? Big boy's mouth was open and sucking in air. The crowd was still crying out, but I did not listen to them anymore. I widened my stance to cover more ground and lowered my left shoulder, ready to receive whatever he had to offer. I took a deep breath and held it. As I waited, I could hear every crunch of his feet on the dirt mixed with the tightened pounding of my heart deep in my chest. Below my armpit, sweat ran down, tempting me to laugh by its tickling gesture. I would have none of it. His arms rose as he began to dive headfirst into me like a linebacker in football. Big boy plowed into me like a tsunami hitting the beach. I could only hope that I held firm. His blow sent me off to the side onto my right elbow; we went down side by side, lying face to face on the fine gravel ground. Dust covered my tongue and clouded my vision. I felt dizzy.

I did not know if I had stopped the run or not. My adversary jumped up and began to walk off to his dugout, as if nothing had happened. His face was expressionless, as if he scored the run but did not want to rub it in my face. A look of despair crossed my face as I realized I may not have stopped him. After several confused seconds, I rolled over to look at the umpire, and he yelled with all he had, "OUT!" The crowd celebrated.

I slowly rose to the cheers of my teammates and coach. My elbow hurt and was bleeding. Our coach was still applauding my effort as he helped me to my feet. He yanked me into his armpit for a half hug as I said, "I hurt my elbow, Coach."

"You'll be fine. You stopped him cold. Good job!"

My team surrounded me, slapped me on the back, and screamed in pure joy. I could hear my mom in the background whooping it up. Clearly, she was insane. For the first time, there was an after game party. I'm sure it was in my honor. The celebration was not like the ones with the Bumblebees, where rainbow drinks and wiggling salads ruled. We, the trailer park team, went to McDonald's. At that moment, there was nothing better than a cheeseburger, fries, and *my* team.

English and I

Masamitsu Murakami

I TRY TO PRONOUNCE the v sound. "Voo Voo Voo." It sounds weird. One of the reasons it sounds weird is that there is no v sound in Japanese language. The other reason is that I try to pronounce the v sound by putting the upper lip to the lower front teeth instead of putting the lower lip to the upper front teeth. "You looked like a bulldog back then," my mother often tells me when she talks about my childhood.

When I was three years old, my family lived in the Kochi prefecture, which is located in southwest Japan. I went to Minori Kindergarten, where English was taught as one of the electives. All I remember are the scenes where I was shown some cards. A drawing was printed on each card. When I was shown each card, I had to say what it was on the card in English. "It's a violin." "It's a tomato." "It's a dog." "It's a cat." Those scenes are now hidden within the shingled, wooden buildings of the kindergarten; however, it is certain that I encountered English in this kindergarten.

One day, when I came back from Osho Elementary school and was watching TV, Chu Arai, a famous comedian in Japan, said abruptly, "This is a pen." He often shouted this phrase out of context. It was a kind of gag. Now, I do not know what was so funny, but back then it was indeed funny and sensational. Almost all children in Japan would mimic him and repeat out of context, "This is a pen." Therefore, most of the children who loved Chu Arai memorized first in their lives "This is a pen." I was one of them. My English teacher was Chu Arai when I was an elementary school student.

In Japan, English education officially begins in junior high schools (though some students start to learn English in elementary schools). When I was a junior high school student, English education meant reading, writing, and grammar. Listening and speaking were never taught. The only sentence I remember from the textbook is "Canada is my country." Why did Canada appear in the textbook? I do not remember. I just recall Mr. Hamada, my English teacher in junior high school, loudly reading the textbook word by word in a Japanese accent while combing his remaining few strings of hair with his right hand.

High school English education in Japan further emphasizes reading, writing, and grammar. This is because students have to prepare for the entrance examinations of universities, which mainly test students' reading, writing, and grammatical knowledge. I do not remember what stories I read and who the teachers were. I just can visualize the teachers scribbling something on the blackboard. I cannot recall their faces. Their silhouettes are fused into the classrooms.

Thanks to these ghost teachers in high school, I was not admitted to any universities. Thus, I ended up going to the Sundai preparatory school, where the students were preparing for the next year's entrance examination. The lessons were of course designed to help students make it to universities; therefore, the English lessons emphasized reading, writing, and grammar. Instructors were just teaching tips to get good scores. Again, I cannot remember their names; I cannot recall their faces. Their figures dissipate into the blackboards.

After being refused by the universities again, I decided to go to the Sundai Foreign Language Institute, where I had American instructors for the first time in my life. At this foreign language institute, I also could learn listening and speaking in addition to reading, writing, and grammar.

One day, Kathy, my writing instructor, complimented me, saying, "You're very good at writing. Why don't you become a technical writer?" I do not know why Kathy recommended that I become a technical writer, but since then the words, "a technical writer," have never come apart from my brain. At that time however, I had no money to pursue a further academic endeavor; therefore, I had to work for a Japanese company for a while.

I worked for Uchimura Inc., which dealt with industrial rubber and resin. The problem was I was the only person who could understand English in that company. Therefore, in addition to the work I had to do as one of the sales representatives, I had to take care of all the documents written in English. Sometimes, the president asked me, "Mr. Murakami, translate this document." Another time, my boss ordered me, "Murakami, translate this brochure." When our company expanded our business to the United States, I had to support one of our staff because he could not understand English at all. When our company established the Indonesian branch, I was in charge of supporting the Indonesian staff because English was the only way to communicate with them. As a result, there were always two towers of documents on my desk. Furthermore, I had to go out to do business with my customers. Before my heart stopped its move, I decided to leave the job. The good news was I had made enough money to study abroad.

Finishing the professional writing program at Missouri State University, I am now a graduate teaching assistant at MSU taking English 603. Dr. Baumlin is talking in front of me; my classmates are surrounding me. I speak, listen, read, and write in English. I am living with English. I try to pronounce the v sound. I think it sounds perfect.

Just Being Practical

Lanette Cadle

THERE I WAS IN MY CAMEL BROADCLOTH JACKET, professionally tousled hair, and contact lenses, joining the crowd of my peers. They were a nice looking bunch. Friendly, tanned to an appropriate turn for the season, necktied or blazered, and ready, really ready to learn. The motivational speaker was one of a happy stream of shiny faces I'd listened to. This one was thirty fiveish, polished, but wise, oh, wise in the ways of salesmanship in ways I would never be. It was at the Kansas State Realtor's® quarterly meeting, and he was making a point.

"Spell Albuquerque," he said. I did it. He smiled, a flicker at one corner only. This was the payoff. "Now spell it backward." The point, I think, was something about brains only taking you so far, or that there are some things no one can do. I'll never know now, because I wrecked the whole setup by spelling Albuquerque backward—without hesitation. The whole presentation skittered a bit at that point, but he was a pro and saved it by asking me how I did that, made sure no one else wanted to try (bubbling laughter from the crowd), and continued on with his spiel. I felt foreign.

Here's how it was done. It's simple. When I spell, I see the word clearly, much like 12 point Courier New on good, heavy rag paper. I then just read it off. Since the word is fully visualized, reading backwards takes a fraction of a second more time, but no more effort. This method has great benefits for classes like Art History as well. All those slides and notes are there, in that pin point visualization spot between the eyes and one inch up, packed up, stored, and ready to view—at least for short term memory. Just like for anyone else, using this method for long term memory takes more effort and upkeep, but for snippets like spelling words, it's unbeatable. Mr. Motivation made sure everyone there knew how it was done and how incredibly uncommon it is. He moved past whatever his point was and switched to deal breaking verbal strategies, how to recognize them, and how to beat them. Back in my seat, I pretended to take notes.

I USED TO READ THE DICTIONARY for fun when I was in elementary school and never told anyone about it, knowing even then that most people would much rather spend their spare time rustling up a dodge ball game or playing cops and robbers on bikes. So would I, at least the nine year old me, but I also had to *know*, and the dictionary was the entrance exam to another world, one I didn't know yet, but one I didn't intend to be excluded from. In the meantime, I read and edited my father's work memos and took typing in summer school.

BEING A REALTOR® IS A good job for a woman who needs to make money, real money. When I began, it was a good way to add a few extra thousand a year to my husband's upwardly mobile income for vacations and frivols. Later, it was a ready method for real money for a single mom of two. Small town America tends to place people in a limited number of categories, and there's only so much room for each one: a few ministers, some lawyers, a sprinkling of small business owners, and a vast morass of consumers in pickup trucks and tank tops on their way to Wal Mart. One of the best lessons in listing I ever got was from my first broker, Ruth. When we were short of listings she would push herself back from her desk and say, "We're almost out of paper towels," and wink. We'd go to Wal Mart and somewhere between the cronies at the snack bar, the housewives checking perfume before school lets out, and the cashiers, she'd get one, sometimes two, appointments with someone who wanted to sell their house. They just didn't know it before she needed paper towels.

For really fast and easy money—and that first year as a single mom I needed it badly—Ruth advised selling mobile homes. In Kansas, mobile homes count as personal property in the same way as vehicles rather than as real property. As long as they aren't on a permanent foundation, the commission is high and the paperwork is low. Even better, the turnaround is lightning fast with a high possibility of a cash sale. Later, when I was a managing broker for another firm, one of the top producers at another branch told me in vivid detail during a car trip to yet another motivational speaker session how easy it is to make money selling cars. He admitted the hours were even worse than real estate (I was working 60–80 hours a week at that point, as were many of my good agents), but spun out a series of nostalgic tales about gullible customers and little to no regulation that shocked what was left of my sales innocence. Easy money, he crooned, and most in the car agreed and chimed in on the mantra.

However, the need to live aside, I still had limits. Selling mobiles was as far as I was willing to go. In the reckless abandon that was the byproduct of buying frenzy, most mobile buyers waived mechanical inspections, trusting their own handyman sense and feeling an aversion to paying anyone to do anything that they could conceivably do themselves. Sometimes this led to nasty phone calls the morning after the first cold snap when the furnace didn't work, but for the most part I felt no guilt. Even without a furnace, those mobiles were their first step toward homeownership and away from an ever more squalid rental life. I felt saintly as I gave them the phone number for a local heating and air firm.

All the same, there were times that I wondered about the, for lack of a better word, "rightness" of what I was doing. Once for a closing gift I gave a giant rubber cockroach to stick on the buyer's refrigerator, in memory of the rental house they left behind; it was so roach infested that the bugs found a way into their refrigerator and danced on the food inside, most likely waggling their little antennae in glee. In order to pass the time while he read the contract, I counted the husband's tattoos, moving up from the roman numerals on his knuckles to the tiny tear drops at the corner of his left eye. When he looked down to read I saw an open eye tattooed on each lid. His wife watched him read, her waist length hair streaked with gray and her face creased with deep lines. She was twenty eight.

IN HIGH SCHOOL I TOOK creative writing for the easy A and found that it was easy, but also found that stopping was not. I wrote the filler poems for the literary journal, the ones that never showed up in submissions, but were needed to make the right rhythm for the reader: poem, poem, poem, drawing, story, poem. I found an old journal a few days ago with a poem fragment in it. The poet at fifteen.

JANUARIES ARE SLOW, AND SOMEONE has to man the phones. I started writing again. Nothing serious, just a little mystery novel to pass the time. It made me look busy when clients came in, which was all for the good. I stopped when I realized that the small moments inside the plot interested me far more than the plot itself. Writing poetry never occurred to me, not even for a moment. I knew no one who read poetry and made the connection that no readers equals no royalty advance. You see, I thought I was going to get paid for writing.

Later, post real estate and after I returned to school, my advisor said, take ESL, you'll always be in demand. I took Intro to Creative Writing for that slot on the English Education degree plan anyway. There wasn't room for any more, though, and my advisor looked down his glasses at me and warned that I would be best served by something more practical.

It was the most practical class I ever took. Sure, the syllabus scared me at first. Carrying the books to my car, I muttered over and over in different rhythms, "Nine poems and two stories. NINE poems and two stories. Nine POEMS and two stories." I never doubted my ability to write the stories, but the poems, the poems. Poetry was alien, a land dreamed of but never inhabited. I wrote the first one, then the next. I said to my instructor, also the coordinator for the MFA program, that I wanted to make money writing and doubted that poetry could do that. He laughed so hard he started wheezing, then he stopped and said, "My God, you're serious," and explained the realities of this writing life. He wouldn't tell me which genre was my strongest, but suggested that I take one more course in each the next semester to find out. There was a course conflict between Nature of Poetry (required) and Fiction Workshop, so Poetry Workshop was the winner. I got it approved by getting a brand new advisor to sign off on my schedule while my regular one was at a conference. Some negotiations work best using sleight of hand.

IT WOULD SOUND MORE NOBLE and fitting if I inserted an epiphany here about how I made the switch to writing. You know—how the heavens part and I slap my forehead hard, shouting "Oy! I should be writing! Enough of this tacky sales life." However, in real life I got canned.

I was managing broker of an office that was yet to make money. My predecessor was a veteran broker, but in her seventies with a penchant for nabbing sales instead of passing them on to agents. There was office unrest, and I was the solution. Unfortunately after four months of trying to recruit more agents and having my efforts shot down by the existing agents who saw the potential influx of seasoned, heavy hitter agents as less business for them, I was out too. I was replaced by a man I had been dating; apparently our breakup was a career move. I held no grudge though, and wished him the best. Offers from four other companies came in within twenty four hours, but I questioned whether diving back in was the right thing to do. I fell back on savings and child support.

Later, when I was through with my B.A. and working on an MFA in Poetry out of state, I heard that he didn't last either. The company owner took over as manager and, surprise, also didn't make the office turn around. My theory that it was a toxic office in a bad location proved true, and the unfortunate result was his bankruptcy and losing all of his offices to an out of town competitor. They immediately closed my former branch. This shouldn't cheer me—but it does.

MY DAUGHTER IS MAKING the rounds of colleges and thinking about majors and what they may or may not lead to. She's picked her school and the housing contract is sent along with a whopping check, so that's settled. The major is a sore spot, though. She's a good writer, a better one than I'll admit to her face. All the same, her first choice for a major was elementary education, despite the fact that she really doesn't like children that much. It was practical, it led to a capital J job in the end, and that was a big concern for her. I don't know what to say. What kind of credibility do I have at this point? I chased dollars with the best of them and put in the hours. She has childhood memories of being my "personal assistant" and coloring at the conference table while I closed a deal. She knows it was just a job and I did it anyway, just like most of the parents of her friends in that small town.

Just being practical sounds good, but needs to be carefully defined. I didn't really face up to my own best self until I realized that money meant little to me compared to the freedom to write and to learn, not only for a few years in school, but for a lifetime. Her best self may be something else, but I pray that she goes for it and ignores the whispers about what is practical and what is not.

I was reading her portfolio at semester's end and marveled at the strong voice and sharp images. Against all odds, she is a poet. She talks about choices, what careers leave time for writing. She also thinks about genres, mourning that poetry pays so little when it pays at all. I say, "So you think someone's going to pay you to write?" This time we both start laughing—gut busting, belly splitting laughter that won't quit until the tears spill down my cheeks, the kind of laughter that hurts where it doesn't show.

Becoming a Biologist

Ryan Edwards

As a Biology major at Missouri State University, I am constantly learning new material. There is not a day that goes by where I am not submerging myself in new vocabulary, trying to interpret a new idea, or formulating the right question for research. This form of literacy, this understanding of scientific method, did not develop overnight. I have spent countless hours each year studying, or even just trying to grasp the subject at hand. It obviously takes patience, determination, and an unceasing source of wonder to keep doing what I do. What some people might not know is that I, along with my peers, have had several specific moments that helped shape who I am today. I did not realize, until I took a recent English class, how much the events in my childhood laid the foundation for what I study today in college.

Throughout my life I have been able to appreciate the hidden messages behind cartoons like the ones found in most newspapers today. They contain simple dialog and artistic and comedic timing to portray a greater message while entertaining the reader. I still flip through textbooks looking for the small cartoons which had little to do with the subject at hand. This love for comics has deep roots in my childhood. My uncle introduced me to *Calvin and Hobbes* when I was nine, maybe ten years old, and I have been hooked ever since. The cartoon is about a little boy and his imaginary tiger who face life's problems and mysteries. As a young boy myself, I quickly became attached to Calvin's harassment of Suzy, his smart and cute next door neighbor, by throwing snowballs and any gross object he could find. I would stay up past my bedtime and read the strips over and over under the covers with my flashlight. Little did I know at the time that I was beginning to ponder the same deep philosophical questions that Calvin was. I believe this kind of questioning I learned as a kid helped shaped me into becoming a biologist.

One might ask, "How did reading *Calving and Hobbes* shape you into becoming a biologist?" Of course, it was not the sole vehicle in my becoming who I am today; as with most things, there were several other factors. What staying up late reading that cartoon did was get me thinking. More importantly, it caused me to think critically, to analyze what I am examining, to break it apart, to dissect the question, to look at it from different angles. This process is very necessary for a biologist to do and is something that has to be learned. For my major, being able to ask the right questions is an expression of literacy.

Calvin would be wandering through his backyard, which happened to be an elaborate forest with wandering streams, cliffs, and abundant wildlife, and then would come across a piece of trash and go into a speech about man's view on nature. Another time, Calvin might be staring at the stars in awe of how big the universe is and wonder why we make such a big fuss over little things. Calvin could always ask the right questions.

Of course, *Calvin and Hobbes* was not my only childhood memory that had an impact on who I am today. Another source was my introduction to the computer. In middle school, my family purchased our first computer, and at the time it was a big deal for me. Games like *SimCity* and *Age of Empires* instantly captured my imagination. No longer was I pretending to lead militaries with little plastic army men; I was a king controlling my civilization through time: finding and exploiting resources for my economy, trading with neighboring colonies for goods, coming up with diplomatic treaties, and even breaking them and going to war. *Age of Empires* was a very complex game, one that required a lot from a young boy. First, I had to know the lingo, which at times was a completely different language. I also had to know how to solve problems: if my civilization needed gold to upgrade its cavalry into paladins, I was the man who had to make it happen. Without my control, my workers would stand around and scratch their butts; it's not their fault they were never properly educated. I decided their fate, I decided what happened, and I could explore the possibilities of experimentation and watch it happen. This helped develop the problem solving skills I use constantly today, as well as paving the way to computer literacy.

America Online (AOL), a dialup Internet access program that has several other features built into it that seemed to be made specifically for kids my age, showed up in my house about the time I was entering seventh grade. My favorite features were the buddy list and instant messaging. The buddy list showed me who was online and who was not. From this window, I could start writing to my friends, and then they could see instantly that I was online, as it popped up on their screens. It was not uncommon for me to be talking to three different people at once for long periods of time. This form of communication, instant messaging, greatly helped my social development and is probably the only reason I can type fluently today. It was not all typing though: AOL showed me the ropes of the computer outside the computer game. It caused me to troubleshoot problems, download and install software, and even understand how a computer works in general. I use these computer skills just as much today as I did ten years ago. In fact, a couple of weeks ago I was trying to use some graphing software, and my computer did not recognize the file type. I knew exactly what it meant and was able to fix the problem. Someone who had yet to receive computer experience might not have been able to understand that. Of course, if I were trying to explain the necessity of computer experience to my parents when I was in middle school, they would have merely laughed.

My parents had a helping hand in my obsession with nature; in fact, some people might say they forced it. Any time I was not doing anything they found productive, I was made to go play outside. At first, it always upset me, because like most kids my age I was rebellious and did not want to do what my parents told me to do. However, it was while I was outside that I first started watching ants carry off sprinkled sugar or birds making nests in trees. It was while I was outside that I released fish into a local pond, and it was while I was outside that I began to love the outdoors. When I started college, I used that love to fuel my desire to understand. Where else is there a better field of study for that purpose than biology?

As I finish up my senior year in college, I cannot help but think of all the things that molded me into who I am today. If Calvin had played inside instead of exploring his world, would I have the ability to question the things I do today? I would like to think I would, but I doubt it. I seriously doubt my interest in the ever increasing problem of stream eutrophication would have surfaced if I never learned how to ask the right questions. Even if it had, the problem requires me to think in a logical order and to understand cause and effect. Did playing *Age of Empires* really help me do that? I think so. I think the computer helped me better formulate the tables, graphs, and reports I use on a daily basis for my studies in biology. This major requires that special form of literacy one can never learn by reading a textbook. It requires the kind of literacy I have just described. I now realize it was this special form of literacy and the love I developed for nature that steered me toward becoming a biologist.

Memoirs of a . . . ?

Erik Renth

I STOOD UP FROM THE PLUSH COMFORT of my seat on the couch. My hands were sweating profusely; that had to be dangerous with the feat I was about to attempt. I cracked my neck and attempted to hold down the bit of fear that was about to escape my stomach. I was crazy for even thinking I could do such a complex action—my body was not built for this! I had watched so many others do it, but surely, I was not one of the people with the athletic ability required to do such a difficult maneuver. I was not even completely sure why I was doing it in the first place; something had just taken over me. At once, I lunged down, put my hands to the bare cement floor, and kicked my legs over my head. "Why the hell am I upside down right now?"—the thought permeated my mind as the alarming idea of falling to an untimely death hit me like a Mack truck. It seemed like forever that I was caught in the abyss of my parallel upside down universe. Suddenly, my feet hit the floor. Wait. Did I just do it? I really had; I had actually done a cartwheel!. I knew plenty of people who would injure themselves just attempting a cartwheel, but I had actually done what I thought was the most difficult thing in the world to do at that moment. It may seem like a very anti climactic moment—all I did was a cartwheel for heaven's sake—but doing my first cartwheel would prove to be the biggest life changing event my then sixteen year old self had ever seen.

By the next day, I had done at least one hundred more cartwheels. I was so enthralled with the tremendous feeling of accomplishment that doing a cartwheel provided. I was very distant from being the most athletic person I knew, so a cartwheel seemed like the epitome of gymnastics maneuvers.

Of course, I would soon learn quite the opposite. I researched a little into gymnastics and found a new skill that I wanted to try—the back handspring. Once I learned about it, I felt like I had to try it. However, several credible sources—Wikipedia is credible, right?—alerted me that the attempt of a back handspring without proper spotting was unadvisable. What do they know? I had to try it regardless of what the "gymnastics experts" on the Internet had to say. I walked outside into the cool grass the next morning, determined to succeed in the same way I had a few days earlier. My toes gripped the dewy blades of grass as I swung my arms over my head and hurled myself backwards at the ground. This time, my upside down time seemed much shorter as my neck hit the wet grass almost immediately. I had finally done it—my stupidity had finally killed me. Well, obviously I did not die, but I was sore for several days after my tragic down*fall*. I obviously could not accomplish my new goal without some sort of help, so I decided to approach the subject cautiously with my parents about trying some tumbling classes. After all, they were expensive, and what would I even be using this tumbling for? Again, with sweating palms—it seems to be a normalcy when I am nervous—I told them I wanted to take gymnastics classes. Surprisingly, they were supportive of my idea to attempt such a unique and unexpected plan; I still do not really understand their motives for encouraging me. Maybe they had known about my horrific accident the previous morning. Maybe they just wanted me to try new things. I decided it was best not to question it.

Two days later, I walked into my first tumbling , still sore from my earlier mishap. I had tossed and turned nervously every night since; I was petrified that I would repeat my fate several times. I cautiously stepped into the massive enclosure of Midwest Twisters Gymnastics with my heart beating a mile per minute—I still get a rush of adrenaline when I walk in. I met my instructor, Kevin, and he asked if I was able to do a cartwheel. Of course, I told him I could do a cartwheel—who could not? What I failed to mention was that I was still scared to death of falling on my head again. Of course, a group of six year old children just happened to be in the gym while I was. All of them were doing back handsprings around me—remind me again why I thought this was a good idea. I do not think I can accurately convey how embarrassed I was at sixteen to be learning how to do a back handspring in a gym filled with toddlers. As with everything in life, however, you must learn to get over it—which I did quickly, because the memory of my tragic back *headspring* easily overcame the embarrassment being in the gym provided. At least I would be safe from neck injury! My instructor and I worked on new drills to improve my coordination and different apparatuses to make the back handspring easier, and somewhere among the moments of embarrassment, problems with injured wrists and toes, and moments of glorious triumph, I actually improved. Before I knew it, I was doing back handsprings by myself—though I did occasionally fall on my head.

Now that I had accomplished my second goal, I had to move on and try something bigger. The next stop was cheerleading. Hold the phone—did I just say cheerleading? Surprisingly, yes. I had always had what some might call an unnatural obsession with my high school's varsity cheerleading squad. It was not a "this call is coming from inside the house" obsession per se; it was more of an "I wish I could do what they are doing" obsession. I was always the loudest fan yelling for the cheerleaders from the stands, and now it was my resolution to join them on the floor. My parents were shocked to say the least. It took quite a bit of adjustment for them to understand my reasoning, but I explained to them that the stereotypes attached to cheerleading were simply no longer accurate. After all, I had accomplished a back handspring, which was required to be a member of the squad, so I felt confident I could make the squad. (So, that statement is an absolute lie. I was so nervous I could hardly sleep at night, but if anyone asked, I was completely cool and collected in regards to the whole situation.) Tryouts for the squad were three weeks away, and I felt like I would never be ready in time. Still, I was firm in my decision to at least attempt to make the squad. I knew if I wanted to save what little pride I had left after my time spent in the gym, I would need to make a miracle happen to improve my skills. I spent nearly all of my free time practicing. I would do handstands to improve my coordination and attempted to do back handsprings in the back yard (a bad idea, trust me.) I would even do toe touches in the garage, watching my form in the reflection of my dad's glossy black truck. I even started practicing with a few of the girls from the squad at tumbling class—things were really looking up. As I began to practice even harder, the thought began to occur to me that I might actually make the squad—I had not really considered the reality of making the squad before. It simply seemed like a far fetched dream I felt very distant from. As I felt myself improving, though, I started feeling more confident that my hard work would actually pay off.

Tryouts arrived, and the days whirled by in a flash of chanting, dancing (yes, I danced) and stunting. Whomever conceived the notion that cheerleaders were pretty faces—however true the case may be—completely missed the fact that cheerleaders work themselves to the bone to accomplish the amazing feats they are required to do on a daily basis. I was dying—the physicality of the activity had truly hit me—and I began to question the necessity of the odd activities they performed. For instance, who came up with the idea that to lead a crowd effectively, a group of cheerleaders must lift a member of their squad over their heads as she contorted her body into uncomfortable positions? Though the concept was completely foreign—and, honestly, just plain silly—I was absolutely enthralled by being a part of it. The feeling of successfully completing a stunt or performing a cheer was electrifying. But wait, what if I did not make the squad— what if this time I did not accomplish my goal? These thoughts hit me again and raced through my mind as I sat on the blue carpeted square I would learn to love as the squad list was posted.

After an eternity of nervous chatter, a bevy of awkward "I hope you make the squad!" moments, and a small group of girls literally breaking down crying, the coach walked in. I vividly remember the next few moments in which she spoke to us as the time seemed to slow to an agonizing pace. I sat partially listening to her talk about how we all did our best and partially picking at the scratchy blue threads that seemed to be assaulting my thighs as I sat on the mat. She droned on for what seemed like forever as I attempted to pretend like I was listening. Finally, she released us to look at the squad roster. The girls on the mat around me rushed for the door; a mess of tears, screams, and joy soon filled the breezeway outside of the gym. I, however, continued to sit on the mat. Calmly, I walked out the door and to the breezeway. Most of the clamor had died down, and I was finally ready to look at the list on my own terms. I had made the squad. A warm rush of energy felt like it washed over me—all was correct in the world. I was truly happy. I had never dreamed that something like cheerleading could make me so fulfilled, but indeed it had.

Jumping forward what seems like an eternity of practices, competitions, games, troubles, and triumphs, I have never regretted the decision I made to become a cheerleader. I have become complete within myself though the lessons I have learned on and off the mat, and I have grown significantly as an individual from contact with the outstanding individuals I have met along the way. Every day I ask myself why the hell I choose to be upside down so much; truthfully, I do not know the answer. Even when I land on my neck, I just cannot seem

42

to give it up. When I feel the need to rationalize my actions, I attribute it to the fact that the passion I feel for cheerleading allows me to push through hardships I would not normally be able to conquer—or at least that sounds rational. Had I never had the courage—or sheer dumb luck—of doing a cartwheel on a whim in my basement, I would be on a very different path in life. For me, a seemingly inconsequential event in life proved to be the most pivotal moment I have ever experienced.

Witnessing Magic

Nancy Mohrlock Bunker

A BOOMING SHOUT, "MAGIC," pierces the raucous crowd inside the Staples Center—professional home to the Los Angeles Lakers, the city's most visible NBA team. In 1999 the arena displaced the beloved Great Western Forum and became the new millennium site for the Lakers 2000, 2001, 2002 three peat championship teams. Dove gray suited Magic Johnson, the Lakers permanent hero, hears his name called and chanted with his every step. A loping gait and smooth casual wave make each person feel as if he is responding to them personally. He searches expectantly into the crowd for the owner's voice. When he looks at you, he gives you complete attention and looks *into* you. Watching him make eye contact with fans explains why folks feel as though they know him.

With a smile that stretches every inch of skin on his face, the constant grin electrifies fans. After the first call out, another voice begs, "Up here, Magic," and another, "We gonna' win, Magic?" as if his word controls destiny. Today, June 10, 2008, the packed audience for Game 3 needs a win to have a chance for the championship. The Lakers dropped the first two games to longtime rivals, the Boston Celtics, and even the most faithful express concern.

Effortlessly slipping into the standard size seat and drawing his legs into a sharp 45 degree angle, Magic has just been freed from a squeezed position in a tall director's chair where he offered commentary with former basketball players and television announcers about this year's Finals. For more than thirty minutes his long legs dangled under him and brushed the floor; large feet rested gingerly on the narrow rest before slipping off. And so he stretched out with gazelle like grace walking away from the glaring spotlight only to find another non media one near his seat.

In every way, he is a big man. At 6 ft. 9 in, he is tall when most stand next to him, his 255 lb. bulk redefines the term critical mass, and his list of basketball accomplishments engenders awe from even his most competitive fellow athletes. The magic of Magic Johnson is often told through statistics, by opponents and teammates, and by Los Angeles Lakers personnel. His career, often delineated by seasons, anchored with numbers, and characterized by records, holds a privileged place in basketball history.

A "phenom" during his high school sophomore year for Lansing, Michigan's Everett High School when his triple double (a term not then coined and one his play made vernacular) spawned his nickname, two years later the senior led his team to a state title win in overtime. As a freshman at Michigan State, he led the Spartans to the Big Ten conference title and a berth in the NCAA Tournament, although his team lost to the Kentucky Wildcats, who ultimately won the 1978 national championship. Magic also brought his team to the NCAA Final game in his sophomore year, and this time defeated Indiana State and won the 1979 Tournament.

Magic Johnson has been a public figure for thirty four years, and I've been watching him for thirty of them. Looking at him folded into a stadium seat today, I recall one of the indelible moments that make up the theatre of his outstanding career. It was those black, black wet eyes just before his November 1991 somber speech. On that sunny California afternoon Magic told the world, "because of the HIV virus I have acquired, I will retire from the Lakers today." Standing at the podium and looking at the faces of dozens of media personnel, he appeared the picture of health. The camera panned the stage to show former teammates wearing dark glasses hiding tear stained faces before shifting priority to the doctors who completed the press conference; their formidable presence verified the facts.

"NO," his fans around the world cried out, "he deserves a chance to avenge the 1990–91 season playoff loss (4–2) delivered by Michael Jordan and the Chicago Bulls. Magic did return to basketball briefly in the 1992–93 season but retired after preseason game controversy. In an unprecedented 1995–96 season, he returned and played power forward for 32 games. Magic averaged 14.6 points, 6.9 assists, and 5.7 rebounds per game at 36 years of age.

Magic's enthusiasm and passion never wane. Here now, in 2008, his eyes express love for the game; he can scarcely sit still. His body language sends every signal that he would relish the NBA Finals opportunity to fight back another time.

As the 2008 Game 3 creeps closer to tip off, I chide myself for not attending to *this* moment. Regardless of the game at hand, sports fans are besieged by memories of players, games, and championships. At a critical time in the 1988 NBA Finals between the Los Angeles Lakers and the Detroit Pistons, I witnessed a unique moment watching Magic that imprinted his spirit on me. Not a public moment, not a moment known to fans, and not a moment recorded on any highlight film. In this defining moment, Magic told his entire story and acted the only narrative anyone needs in order to learn about success: it is all in the timing.

The Lakers had given up their home court advantage in a game one 105–93 loss. The *LA Times* taunted the NBA's winningest team of the 80s wondering in print whether the Lakers possessed a style built on blood, guts, and courage as the Pistons seemed to be. The flashy, Hollywood, "Showtime" reputation inferred that the Lakers win with sleight of hand rather than with extraordinarily talented, fundamentals driven, and dauntless team players.

At 3 p.m., June 1988, it is three hours before Game 2, and I walk down a dark, empty, and silent hallway leading to the

Great Western Forum arena. Even the sound of my shoes on the tile intrudes. No strobe lights, no big voiced announcers, no blaring music, no acrobatic dancers, and no fans, yet. The single light comes from a filtered ray shining from the ceiling casting a haze over the playing floor. The pitch black stands—floor to rafters—encircle the 17, 505 seats, all empty.

I sat alone with spectator anticipation and cautious optimism for a Lakers win. My eyes linger on the varnished flooring that produced my memories of this team's legendary spectacular moments—ones that put the larger than life franchise into the record books.

I replay Magic playing guard, forward, and center at different times in the crucial game six of his 1979 rookie season. The Lakers defeated the Philadelphia 76ers in four games and won the NBA Championship in a Finals characterized by the stuff that dreams are made of.

I can see the 1985 stalwart Kareem Abdul Jabbar's Game 2 and Game 5 that forced the series 3–2 lead; Magic's 15 assists per game average in the Finals crushed the Boston Celtics in six games.

I remember Magic's "junior, junior, junior Sky hook" produced the game winning shot that put the Lakers up three to one and coined for the 1987 Finals a new phrase in basketball's lexicon. The Lakers went on to win in six games over the Celtics.

Those history making games took on a life of their own after championship wins, I told myself, and the 1998 Lakers can do it again this year. CBS Sports broadcasters busily write copy for the network's opening comments on tonight's broadcast and stay clear of the playing floor. Pat O'Brien's upbeat feature will glamorize the celebrity fans by pointing out a "star seating" diagram to television audiences. He ignores the Lakers loss. Only one game down, and the media's gloomy thinking weighs heavily. Here in the cavernous arena all seats look the same, and the not famous can dare to take a space where a celebrity will sit once the game begins.

My eyes scan the empty space. The court appears double its size without players and without activity. Basketball is a game of constant motion and frenetic, controlled plays. Without the game, the court is simply a floor. Children and adults play virtually the same game. It may be sacrilege for the die hard professional sport fan to accept, but remarkable universality and equality exist even among disparate playing levels. Pre game hours occur before every basketball contest, and the same quiet time might precede any basketball game, between any two teams, in any city, and for any stakes.

The Great Western Forum looks dismal. No easily recognizable players amble through routine practice sets, no season MVP hears thunderous applause, no chic coach saunters to his history making team at the players' bench. The sky hooks, lightening flash steals, and no look passes characterizing Showtime lie dormant. Guesses hang in the air.

Earvin Magic Johnson is one of those guesses. Not only was his performance in Game 1 not as expected but also in the pre dawn hours of the following morning he awakened with the flu. He showed up for practice and struggled through initial drills before being sent home. For the past 58 hours, Magic has been battling the flu, and the flu is winning. The energy sapping monster debilitated this finely tuned athletic machine; the Lakers trainer describes Magic as wobbly. Unable to sleep or eat, the press hints at the Unthinkable . . . the Inexpressible. Maybe Magic will not play Game 2. The dark and empty arena breeds the obvious fear. Maybe the Lakers will not come back. Maybe they will not be the 1988 NBA champions.

Then, a shadow walks out of the darkness. An adolescent young man clad in Lakers gold "home" practice clothes emerges from the locker room tunnel. He carries a basketball securely positioned at his waist and stops just inside the nearest court corner. His fingers tap the ball, his feet shuffle, his eyes dart over the dark rows of sets. Even the ball boy shows palpable nerves.

Instinctively, my eyes squint and pierce the void at the mouth of the tunnel. The reason for the young man's skittishness is the figure with head down and arms limp taking measured steps toward the court. In obvious pain, Magic Johnson moves into the haze. Face ashen, stride weak, a body lighter by 13 pounds than two days before appears more grim than the press report. This man bears no resemblance to the player on television. He is not running, not sweating, not taking interview questions, and not smiling.

Stopping at a spot on the court and making one nearly imperceptible wrist gesture, Magic signals his young helper to stand in a specific place. Silently and swiftly the sneakered feet take their assigned position. Holding his hands waist high, Magic nods, the young man lobs the ball. Private practice begins. I hold my breath with the first half dozen shots stifling a fear that this ill giant will drop to the floor. Neither the young man nor I or even both of us together possess the strength to drag Magic's 6 feet 9 inch, 210 lb. pound body to the locker room.

Eyes fixed on the hoop, Magic's every movement provides a clinic in efficiency. The bounce shoot, bounce hesitate shoot, pass shoot, impeccably timed rhythms meld experience with training. Continually fed the ball, Magic steps, jumps, dribbles, fakes, and falls away. Any and every shot he might take in the game he takes now. He repeated each sequence so many times I lost count.

Technique governed. He visualizes his opponents, imagines their defense; he knows that in game two he will be overtly pressured and covertly bumped. He will be elbowed and jabbed. He will be hacked. He will be knocked down.

Moving slightly an arm, a shoulder, a foot, both feet, he took a myriad of variations on the same shot. Again and again and again. He never looked away from the goal. He shot basket after basket with total concentration while I silently counted ten, then seven, next twelve, and then fourteen consecutively made shots. Every time the ball left his hands, the shot looked like a reflex.

The practicing player manifested none of the toothy, "havin' fun" hero expected when the Lakers play. Magic's familiar responses, "just taking it one game at a time" . . . "playing our kind of ball" . . . "we know what we have to do," satisfy reporters, and they are always coupled with a smile. No smiling now. Practice. Period.

Magic looked less tall alone on the court without his teammates, less strong in practice garb, less the star sans applause, and much less like the game's Magic Man. But here in the solo work of practice is where the magic is to be found— in the fundamental concept of preparation. Bodily strength increases and mental intensity recovers through consistent practice. Driven to excellence, the nine year veteran brought himself onto the court three hours before game two to assess his ability to play. A voyeur, I take a measure of the man.

Some time later, Magic's boyhood friend and current opponent for the NBA Championship, Isaiah Thomas, stepped onto the court, caught Magic's ball after it passed through the net, and sent it back to him. Their eyes met, and they exchanged a smile as Magic stepped behind the 3 point line. He took a jump shot that swished easily. When the young helper returned the ball, Magic passed it back. Private practice was over.

He ran slowly the perimeter of the court three times, he ran backward up and down the court two times, and he left by the same dark tunnel that gained him entry. Silently, the Magician disappeared.

Alone again in the wake of the moment, I recounted the situation. It had taken a season of 100 games and two 7 game series against the Utah Jazz and the Dallas Mavericks to reach the Finals with the Pistons. The possibilities existed that other teammates would have an off night, another world class player would sustain an injury; maybe this series would go seven games.

"A Sick Magic Did the Trick" headlined the *LA Times* after the Lakers Game 2 two victory. Seeing him up close, off camera, alone, and scrutinizing his every move, I believed then that he alone held the team's destiny within him. He has said, "Playing to win, that's all I'm about," and that means intensity and emotion coupled with poise and control. Such a statement is code for Flawless Timing. Coach Pat Riley's words echoed: effort is what separates 1 year champs from teams of lasting greatness. And so he brought his determination, precision, and consistency. He gave more than 100% even when there wasn't 100% to give. Witnessing Magic Johnson practice before Game 2 crystallized my belief that the Lakers would cement their legacy. He knew what it would take for his team to win it all. They did. Magic's name may conjure up the unseen, but his work ethic is completely visible.

Amidst the wild celebration and story book summer no one knew and no one could have predicted these championship games would constitute the pivotal last moment in Magic's illustrious career. The moment I saw set the ground for the series and the Lakers rallied.

The 1988 Finals were the last Lakers championship in the decade, the last championship played by Magic and his Showtime teammates, and the last of the 80s history making franchise.

A horn blast jars me back to 2008, and the Staples Center noise level escalates to deafening. I watch Magic's eyes as he takes in every pass, squints at every missed basket, and closes his eyes with every made three point shot. The arena sound precludes any conversation, so I return to my memories of this man who has never appeared ill.

Barely three months after his separation announcement, on February 16, 1992, the Lakers franchise retired Magic's number 32 jersey. Tiers of fans standing on tiptoes in the stands craning their necks glimpsed the man in his dress suit, who after he took the microphone, quietly commented and tearfully looked into the eyes of every speaker who spoke about him. To a person, tears brimmed every speaker's eyes when Magic addressed him. His voice broke, I recall, much in the same way it did when he announced his retirement. Friends and family standing on the court floor positioned themselves in a wide semi circle at the start of the dedication ceremony. Speakers stepped forward a few feet and told their personal Magic stories. After completing his remarks, each speaker returned to his place. What was so powerful to observe was the semi circle's gradual and nearly imperceptible tightening until the speakers gradually engulfed Magic.

From fifteen feet away, it was as though the membership on the court floor decided to form a Roman Turtle around him, buffer whatever came to take him, fight for him and with him, and if possible, protect him from harm. Many many people, most of them strangers, wept openly for the loss of this man to the game, but the tears were also fears, fears he would lose his life. Grappling with collective concern melded the televised audience and witnesses at the Great Western Form that Sunday afternoon.

In August 1992 the robust Magic and the original Dream Team won the Olympic gold medal. With a face wreathed in a smile and soaked with tears, Magic later said this was the most important moment of his career. Magic refused to let the Nike Reebok controversy over warm up suit logos detract from his pride. Cloaking himself in the American flag, the man who had amassed a professional resume unparalleled by any in his field wore the win on his shoulder and his feelings on his sleeve. His eyes never blinked during the *Star Spangled Banner*, and when applause roared, his gaze fixed upon the flag worn with awe and reverence.

Being named to the Naismith Hall of Fame, Magic said, became his important career moment. In 2002, he was introduced at the ceremony by Boston Celtics Larry Bird, his career rival and personal friend. Magic's eyes never left Bird's face. Hearing the history of accomplishments, records set, statistics recalled, and contests revisited Magic's winsome smile dissolved into a solemn visage. Bird spoke of them both entering the NBA in 1979 and Magic's eyes glistened with tears I remembered reading that Bird said the first thing he looked at after every game was Magic's box score; everything else was unimportant. Magic told everyone who would listen that the season consisted of 80 regular games and "the two" against the Celtics. They developed as professionals and played while both were at the peak of their careers. Revitalizing interest in the game was a byproduct of their relentless unconditional competition. They fought for the same college championships for two years and strove for the same professional championships for thirteen years. As he took the podium, the complete and complex respect in Magic's smile was one that perhaps only Bird understood.

As the Staples Center crowd rises to its feet for the singing of the National Anthem June 2008, Magic unfolds himself from the seat, takes up the stance of his playing days, and instinctively sways side to side. He has had a dozen years to become accustomed to watching subsequent Lakers teams, but he has not adjusted to the physical excitement coursing through his body before the game begins.

Magic Johnson's career has been marked by the visual images on *Sports Illustrated* covers, ESPN *Classic* TV basketball video footage, and global newspaper photos. Hundreds of pictures from his life can be found on the internet, and his rookie collectable trading card can be purchased on ebay. Advocacy as an AIDS spokesman guarantees being photographed when he testifies on Capitol Hill. A life size billboard appeared in the Washington DC train stations during the summer of 2008 with his encouragement to become involved in one's neighborhood.

A man with heart larger than his body, basketball talent that exceeds his playing years, and an understanding of the game that distances even the most accomplished sport knowledge; he is not for an age, but for all time. Magic, the professional basketball player and Ben Jonson's comments about Shakespeare probably have not shared the same sentence before now. Their names do not appear together in *Sports Illustrated* or *The Norton Shakespeare*, and the very idea of placing them with each other may strike basketball fans as contrived and literary scholars as ludicrous. True, they are an unlikely pair, but similarity lies in their ability to make the most of their time.

Magic is one of the very few players whose amazing individual skills changed the way the game is played; he lives in a celebrity milieu in the real world. Shakespeare is one of a handful of playwrights whose dramatic figures boast nearly five hundred years of diverse critical interest while inhabiting fictional spaces in the world of the play. Both men narrate stories that reveal and reflect our innermost human nature, capturing world wide recognition that touches even the most the peripheral sports fan or casual theatre goer. What is telling is that Shakespeare's tragic heroes succumb to negative circumstances and lose all sense of time while Magic, buoyed by the negative, sharpens his timing and survives to fight another day.

Appendix

Career Highlights:
- NCAA Championship (1979)
- NCAA Tournament Most Outstanding Player (1979)
- Los Angeles Lakers Career: 13 years
- NBA Champion (1980, 1982, 1985, 1987, 1988)
- NBA Most Valuable Player (1987, 1989, 1990)
- NBA All-Star (1980, 1982, 1983, 1984, 1985, 1986, 1987, 1988, 1989, 1990, 1991, 1992)
- NBA Finals MVP (1980, 1982, 1987)
- All-NBA First Team (1983, 1984, 1985, 1986, 1987, 1988, 1999, 1990, 1991)
- All-NBA Second Team (1982)
- NBA All-Star Game MVP (1990, 1992)
- Olympic Gold Medal Basketball Team (1992)
- NBA's 50th Anniversary All Time Team (1996)
- Naismith Memorial Hall of Fame (2002)
- California Sports Hall of Fame (2007)

Real Stones and False Beauty

Nancy Walker

THE MUD WAS PERFECT, just creamy enough to look like chocolate to a four year old, crouching in the back yard on a summer day when the bees buzzed lazily. I dipped one stone in the mud. Carefully. When the stone was mud covered, I set it on the bottom porch step. Then I dipped another. And another. Soon I had a dozen mud covered stones. As I dipped the thirteenth, my aunt came out the back door.

"Auntie, would you like some chocolate candy?" I asked.

"Thank you. I'd love some."

My favorite aunt sat on a porch step, picked up one of the stones, and put that pretend candy in her mouth. I waited for her to spit out the stone. She didn't. I cried.

"Auntie, Auntie, that was a mud covered stone, not candy."

She put her arms around me and said, "Honey, I didn't really eat the stone, I just pretended."

Pretending is a wonderful childhood occupation. I always have thought imaginary playmates were a delightful idea. As a child, I pretended that a rock formation in the mountains was a country inn. And that was delightful. Such fictions enrich a child's world, help a child see possibilities.

Adults need to see the danger in pretending with children, though. Children should be in charge of their fictional worlds, and adults shouldn't appropriate a child's fictions. My well meaning aunt should have made an elaborate show of pretending to pretend to eat the mud covered stone. Her realistic act changed the plot of my fiction and threatened my understanding of pretending. My fantasy truth—the plot my aunt violated—ended with my knowing all along she was pretending, ending with our laughing together at a delicious joke. Instead, I cried.

These days, I hear that young people have no "creativity." They don't know how to use their imaginations. Of course, the loss of an active imagination can have many causes. I wonder, though, whether some young people had unfortunate experiences when they were children. Perhaps some children decided that pretending was dangerous because, after all, Auntie could have believed the story was true, could really have eaten the stone. Pretense has its own rules of "truth," rules that are careful about real stones in imaginary gardens.

I wonder about the implications for teaching children to write. We know we want them to brainstorm before they write, to discover what they want to say. Teachers need to be able to ask questions without violating the children's pretending, their plots. Recently, I read a second grader's story about "The Day I Was Two Inches Tall." When I came to a statement about having to eat "ant stew." I was enchanted. What a wonderful imagination, I thought. Then I read another child's story about the same experience. That child, too, referred to "ant stew." I realize they may have been sitting beside each other as they wrote. Perhaps one of them said, "If I were two inches tall, I'd prob'ly have to eat ant stew." Perhaps the other said, "That's neat. I'll have to eat ant stew, too." On the other hand, the idea for ant stew may have come from the brainstorming session led by the teacher. If so, the teacher may have—unknowingly, of course—tampered with the children's imaginations.

To avoid accidental tampering, teachers could take the children on a guided fantasy, asking them, "Now that you're two inches tall, what do you look like? Where do you live?

What do you do for fun? What do you eat?" Students would gather their ideas silently so that each response would be genuinely individual. Of course, even asking the questions imposes the adult's vision of being two inches tall on the children. We probably can't avoid some amount of imposing on them, but we can remember how fragile the childlike imagination is, how devastating too much adult reality can be on that imagination.

The ghost of real stones in imaginary gardens can haunt us when we respond to children's writing, too. That is, we can intrude on children's written stories the way my aunt intruded on my living story. In conferences, listening to children tell us what they want to say and how they want to say it usually is far more helpful than telling them what we want to read.

"Four eyes, four eyes, ugly old four eyes." Those strangers were shouting at me. I had wire rimmed glasses in the days when almost no children wore glasses. I was four years old. I was cross eyed.

I rushed up the front steps of my grandparents' house, slammed the door, and ran to the room I always stayed in when we visited. I took off my glasses and knuckled away the tears. They wouldn't stop. Then came the chest quaking sobs that I couldn't stop, either. My aunt came into the room, put her hand lightly on my shoulder, and said, "Nancy Lou, what's the matter?"

I swallowed a sob and said, "They said I'm ugly."

"Who?"

"Those kids outside."

"Well, what do they know? You and I know you're beautiful."

I sobbed harder. Not only was I ugly: my aunt had just lied to me. Eventually, she left. Then came Grandma, then Grandpa, then Mama. All of them assured me I was beautiful.

I knew better.

These days, I wonder about the undoubtedly loving family, telling a cross eyed child with a fuzzy Toni permanent, "You're beautiful." Even a four year old knows what the mirror says. Their pretense was meant to comfort me, of course. Instead, their pretense threatened my understanding of truth.

I wish that they had said, "You're beautiful because your kindness makes me feel good."

"You're beautiful because you make me laugh."

"I like the way you look."

Or something about kinds of physical beauty. Or something.

As children, we were told to tell the truth. "Yes, I peeled the wallpaper in my bedroom." "Yes, I broke the window." Adult exhortations to tell the truth assume, however, that the truth is simple when, in fact, much truth is complex. Truth about wallpaper and windows is simple. Truths about beauty are not. When adults tell a comforting lie, they confuse children about "truth." I could have told my family, "I thought you said always tell the truth." But I didn't.

Always tell the truth. What does that mean when we respond to children's writing? We should be like the children who shouted "Ugly old four eyes," but we shouldn't be like my family, either. My family, by commenting on the value of my kindness or sense of humor, could have helped me move toward a sense of personhood. We, by making careful (and truthful) comments and by asking questions of our writers, can help them develop a sense of authorship. No authors will emerge if we criticize minute problems. No authors will emerge if we blindly praise everything. Lucy Calkins sometimes tells students, "I like the beginning—the ending is less good" (121). That's truth telling.

Work Cited

Calkins, Lucy McCormick. *The Art of Teaching Writing*. Portsmouth, NH: Heinemann, 1986.

Chapter Two:

Sourced Writing

Sovereign Wealth Funds: Implications for National Security and Stability

Ryan McGinness

With a steady stream of news stories lately, the issue of sovereign wealth funds (SWF) is gaining the attention of legislators, regulators, and commentators. Given that many are uncomfortable with the notion of any sovereignty owning significant portions of industries considered vital to national interests, it is important to examine the issue in a sober manner with a realistic appraisal of any potential threats from SWFs. The threats posed to national security by sovereign wealth funds are small, inherently constrained, and require a very specific parlay of circumstances. In light of this, any ill measured reaction would undoubtedly cause more harm than good.

Introduction

Sovereign wealth funds are investment funds owned by foreign governments, first created in the 1950's by oil and natural resource producing nations to stabilize their currencies and economies against fluctuations in commodity prices or invest for future generations.[1] Since then, twenty SWFs in excess of $10 billion have been created, holding $2.032 trillion in assets, more than the private hedge fund market.[2] The largest SWFs include the Abu Dhabi Investment Authority of the United Arab Emirates ($500B–$800B), the Government of Singapore Investment Corporation ($100B–$300B), and the Government Pension Fund of Norway ($308B).[3] The current size of SWFs is significant, and they are here to stay. A Morgan Stanley study finds that by 2015 SWF assets could reach over $12 trillion.[4] America's brand of capitalism is confronted with significant dissonance between its concept of governments' role in economies and the reality of large and growing state controlled funds. Without a reconciliation of our impression of state involvement in foreign investment and the reality of today, there is a danger of nationalistic backlash that could result in the impediment of capital flows.

The concept of sovereign wealth funds actually predates the term used today to discuss policy; the first fund was created in 1953 by Kuwait.[5] While an exact definition of sovereign wealth funds is an elusive one, Stephen Jen offers the most precise, citing five characteristics exhibited by all sovereign funds: "sovereign government entities, high foreign currency reserves, no explicit liabilities (such as a pension fund), high risk tolerances, and long investment horizons."[6]

Funds meeting these criteria are generally established for three distinct but non exclusive reasons: stabilization funds, savings funds, and the investment of foreign reserves. The boundaries between each purpose are not bright dividing lines, the purposes of a particular fund may be mixed or even change over time as sovereignty's economic circumstances change. Alternatively, many countries establish multiple funds, each to serve a different purpose. However, SWF owning countries that are disconcerting to policymakers are secretive, not disclosing even the purpose or investment aims of a fund, much less the assets and activities of said funds. The unnecessary secrecy and lack of clear purpose limits the ability to gauge the fund's intent and the exposure of a host country. Regardless of a fund's exact purpose, the national security risks are essentially the same. However, the purpose is relevant as it affects the investment strategy; stabilization funds have the most limited and risk adverse investment philosophy, and foreign reserve funds are afforded the most flexibility in investment horizon and risk tolerance. The stabilization funds are most limited because their primary purpose is macroeconomic and currency stabilization, they need access to highly liquid assets that are readily available for use. Savings funds are designed for intergenerational transfers of wealth, or essentially the conversion of non renewable resources into assets. This approach will tend to emphasize income producing assets over time as natural resources are depleted and new streams of revenue are obtained. Funds that are simply seeking higher returns on foreign reserves are the most flexible, for the simple reason that they are beholden to no purpose besides maximizing returns on investment. This implies a small degree of liquidity is required, and thus these funds are able to invest however they please. The wide range of options available to SWFs funded by foreign reserves make them the most potentially threatening.

Significance

It is the issue of transparency that is of paramount concern to regulators: with transparency then any would be malicious funds have little ability to pose a threat to stability. In order for a SWF to maneuver itself into a position to threaten the interests of the United States, it must first obtain at least a significant if not a controlling stake in a firm that is uniquely important to national security. This limits firms of interest to those in a defense, infrastructure, telecommunications, or perhaps a financial field. Beyond that, there must be a uniqueness to the firm such that the interests of the United States could not be quickly and easily served by another firm. This in itself is an unlikely proposition, given the strong outcry over a 2007 attempt by the United Arab Emirates' DP World to purchase several large U.S. shipping ports.[7, 8] According to testimony given before the Senate Banking, Housing, and Urban Affairs Committee by Edwin Truman, only 8 of 24 countries with SWF have direct equity stakes in firms of foreign origin, or even consider direct equity as part of their investment repertoire.[9] Even if one of these SWF were to obtain a controlling stake in a unique firm of U.S. interest, the actions of the sovereignty would be constrained by those options that are economically viable. Remembering that the assets of these funds are large and significant, it is difficult to imagine a scenario that enables a fund to subjugate economic considerations to strategic and political ones without completely destroying the value of its assets.

Despite the high hurdles to obtaining control of a firm, there are still worries of potential conflicts of interest and improper use of influence gained by investment. The lack of reciprocal access to markets and heavy investment of a SWF in strategic industries only exacerbates these concerns. In addition to these, corporate governance, state capitalism, and economic and industrial espionage concern policymakers and regulators. Reciprocal access is a key component of a sensible policy on foreign direct investment; but should we not be granted access to foreign markets that would not be sufficient justification to deny them their desire to invest in our markets. If they should throw rocks in their harbor, should we fill ours as well? Foreign investment that may or may not be welcomed in reverse still provides the U.S. with capital inflows that lower interest rates, create American jobs and spur domestic economic growth. We should welcome foreign investment regardless if our investment would be welcome there.

It is not hard to make the small leap from protectionist policies of investor nations to potential state capitalists. A legitimate concern is that those who would bar foreign investment yet desire stakes in strategic sectors would use their newly found influence to favor their state controlled corporations and pursue economic or political power. Any use, or even the perception of the possibility of use of state owned firms in the energy sector for political purposes, will have a strong destabilizing effect on those economies and decrease efficiency of those markets. Any hypothetical government involved in the management of their SWF will know this; and the negative consequences of market instability is enough reason to "threaten the threat", if you will. The less involved the political leadership is in the management of the SWF, the less likely politicization of markets and resources is to occur, and is one of many benefits of independent management and oversight of SWFs.

Among other difficulties with the oversight of SWFs is the issue of corporate governance. Securities regulations are incredibly complex with a high cost of enforcement and compliance, and vary widely from country to country. Ensuring compliance with such laws is virtually impossible as of now; it would be difficult to even know if a country is being cooperative with our requests to enforce SEC regulations, as our jurisdiction ends abruptly at our borders. SEC chairman Christopher Cox raises concerns of a conflict of interest between countries operating SWFs but responsible at the same time for investigating fraud and insider trading. There is also the possibility of SWFs benefitting from "economic intelligence" gathered by foreign intelligence agencies.[10] It is a well known principle that free markets thrive on freely available and accurate information; introduction of such asymmetric information will undoubtedly decrease market efficiency and stability, especially considering the massive size of these economic actors. The scope of these concerns is wide, applying to all investments that a SWF makes in a host country. This makes this issue one to watch; while not an issue today it would be preferable that policymakers got in front of these potential conflicts before they are realized.

Even if these foreign governments do not directly defy corporate governance regulations, some are concerned about increased access to sensitive information should a SWF become involved in an American firm. It should be noted that this is largely predicated on the condition that a SWF holds a significant or controlling stake in the firm, enough to perhaps imperceptibly steer a firm into circumstances that would prove more advantageous. As previously mentioned, there is some implausibility of this scenario, but furthermore, these risks are non unique to sovereign wealth funds.[11] While the creation of diffuse networks of personal relationships will certainly be a consequence of increased cross border holdings, several countries have proved to be skillful at industrial espionage without the involvement of SWFs, especially China.[12] On the flip side of this coin, these diffuse networks are also part of a broader social agenda of some SWFs, which is to increase their access to human capital and the sophistication of their financial markets. The strong pattern of investment in major American financial institutions is an excellent case study of this effort, with about $40 billion invested in the U.S. financial sector in 2007 alone.[13]

Current Policy

There are currently government policies and mechanisms to ensure direct foreign investment does not threaten national security. Other concerns of conflicts of interest and political objectives are not addressed, however. The Committee on Foreign Investment in the United States (CFIUS) evaluates any foreign investments that potentially impact national security. The application process for investment is voluntary, but widely abided by as foreign investors remain subject to divestment at any time if they do not submit an application. CFIUS makes a non binding recommendation to the President, who has the final decision in the matter.[14] However, since most SWF transactions involve non controlling stakes or non voting shares and CFIUS only has jurisdiction over industries specifically related to national security, it is unclear how much of SWF activity is subject to review.[15] In July 2007 H.R. 556: Foreign Investment and National Security Act was passed into law. This expands the scope of sectors considered relevant to national security and is sufficient for blocking the acquisition of direct equity stakes by SWFs or other state controlled entities, but does nothing to address less immediate issues of conflicts of interest and statist capitalism.[16]

It is nearly certain that to address the less immediate concerns the proliferation of SWFs an international consensus must be reached on a set of best practices to ensure transparency and minimal financial stability risks. Fortunately, our European allies share our concerns regarding SWFs. The reaction of Western Europe runs from reactionary positions led by German PM Angela Merkel[17] and French President Nicolas Sarkozy[18] to a more reasonable position taken by the United Kingdom.[19] The positions taken by France and Germany are fueled in large part by their dependence on Russian natural gas supplies, which contribute to a large part of their energy infrastructure, particularly Germany.[20] While the rhetoric is unhelpful, it is more understandable in light of the recent spinoff of $35 billion from the Stabilization Fund of the Russian Federation to create a new SWF with a more aggressive investment strategy.[21]

Establishing a set of international best practices to ensure the interests of both host countries and those possessing SWFs would be ideal. The International Monetary Fund would be the best avenue to develop this set of best practices. While no SWF countries are borrowers from the IMF and thus not subject to their requirements, most are members and have committed to conduct conducive to international stability. Edwin Truman concisely defines the categories that these best practices should cover: structure of the SWFs, governance, transparency and reporting, and behavior.[22] Clearly defined funding structures and rules governing the usage of funds without frequent alteration would illuminate the structure of SWFs. Clear establishment of the role of the government in setting the investment strategy and preferably, independence of the management of a SWF from the political leadership would ensure that the funds do not act in a non commercial manner. Frequent reports of fund activity, returns, and assets would provide transparency and confirm the stated goals and investment philosophy of funds. Lastly, public disclosure of a fund's behavior regarding the use of leverage (e.g. debt, derivatives) and consultation of large investments or divestments that may affect the host countries currency and economic stability is desirable. Clearly an establishment of such best practices would be in our interest, due to our role as a host country. Such an agreement would also relieve concerns and prevent an unnecessary erection of barriers to capital flows. The efforts of the IMF, the World Bank, and the Organization for Economic Cooperation and Development (OECD) to host a dialogue between host countries and SWF countries are encouraging; however, ultimately it is the countries possessing SWFs that must decide that adopting and adhering to these practices is in their best interests.

Bibliography

Aizenmann, Joshua, and Reuven Glick. "Sovereign Wealth
Funds: Stumbling Blocks or Stepping Stones to Fi
nancial Globalization?" Federal Reserve Bank of San
Francisco Economic Letter, No. 2007–38. December 14,
2007.

"Darling says sovereign funds need to follow rules." *Reuters*.
October 22, 2007.

Jackson, James K. "The Exon Florio National Security Test
for Foreign Investment." *CRS Report RL33312*. Wash
ington D.C.: Congressional Research Service, July 28,
2006.

Jen, Stephen. "Currencies: How Big Can Sovereign Wealth
Funds Be by 2015," *Morgan Stanley Global Research*,
May 3, 2007.

Kramer, Andrew E.. "Russia Creates a $32 Billion Sovereign
Wealth Fund." *New York Times*. February 1, 2008, Busi
ness Section. http://www.nytimes.com/2008/02/01/busi
ness/worldbusiness/01fund.html?_r=1&oref=slogin
(accessed May 6, 2008.)

Rothnie, David. "Sovereign wealth spending on banks ex
ceeds $50bn," *Financial News Online,* January 14, 2008.

Shambaugh, David. "The 'China Honeymoon' Is Over."
International Herald Tribune, November 26, 2007. http://
www.iht.com/articles/2007/11/26/opinion/edsham
baugh.php?WT.mc_id=rssfrontpage (accessed May 6,
2008.)

Truman, Edwin M. "Sovereign Wealth Fund Acquisitions
and other Foreign Government Investment In the
United States." Testimony before U.S. Senate, Commit
tee on Banking, Housing, and Urban Affairs. November
14, 2007.

Weiss, Martin A. "Sovereign Wealth Funds: Background
and Policy Issus for Congress." *CRS Report RL34336*.
Washington D.C.: Congressional Research Service,
January 31, 2008.

Notes

[1] Martin A. Weiss, *CRS Report RL34336* (Congressional Research Ser vice, 2008), CRS 1.

[2] Ibid, CRS 10.

[3] Edwin M. Truman, "Sovereign Wealth Fund Acquisitions and other Foreign Government Investment In the United States." Testimony be fore U.S. Senate, Committee on Banking, Housing, and Urban Affairs. November 14, 2007.

[4] Stephen Jen, "Currencies: How Big Can Sovereign Wealth Funds Be by 2015," *Morgan Stanley Global Research*, May 3, 2007.

[5] Martin A. Weiss, *CRS Report RL34336* (Congressional Research Ser vice, 2008), CRS 1.

[6] Ibid, CRS 6.

[7] Joshua Aizenmann and Reuven Glick. "Sovereign Wealth Funds: Stum bling Blocks or Stepping Stones to Financial Globalization?" Federal Re serve Bank of San Francisco Economic Letter, No. 2007–38. December 14, 2007.

[8] One must wonder at the real security threat in this scenario; does a ter rorist really need to buy the port to smuggle weapons or supplies through it?

[9] Edwin M. Truman, "Sovereign Wealth Fund Acquisitions and other Foreign Government Investment In the United States." Testimony be fore U.S. Senate, Committee on Banking, Housing, and Urban Affairs. November 14, 2007.

[10] Martin A. Weiss, *CRS Report RL34336* (Congressional Research Ser vice, 2008), CRS 16.

[11] Recalling the example of the UAE ports deal, does a foreign country really need to acquire a stake in a firm in order to conduct industrial or economic espionage?

[12] David Shambaugh. "The 'China Honeymoon' Is Over." *Interna tional Herald Tribune*, November 26, 2007. http://www.iht.com/arti cles/2007/11/26/opinion/edshambaugh.php?WT.mc_id=rssfrontpage (accessed May 6, 2008.)

[13] David Rothnie, "Sovereign wealth spending on banks exceeds $50bn," *Financial News Online,* January 14, 2008.

[14] James K. Jackson. "The Exon Florio National Security Test for Foreign Investment." *CRS Report RL33312*. July 28, 2006.

[15] Martin A. Weiss, *CRS Report RL34336* (Congressional Research Ser vice, 2008), CRS 16.

[16] Ibid.

[17] Marcus Walker. "Germany Tinkers With Foreign Takeovers Plan."

Wall Street Journal. A2, January 14, 2008.

[18] "Sarkozy attacks wealth funds on eve of Mideast trip." *Reuters.* January 12, 2008.

[19] "Darling says sovereign funds need to follow rules." *Reuters.* October 22, 2007.

[20] Marcus Walker. "Germany Tinkers With Foreign Takeovers Plan." *Wall Street Journal.* A2, January 14, 2008.

[21] Andrew E. Kramer. "Russia Creates a $32 Billion Sovereign Wealth Fund." *New York Times.* February 1, 2008, Business Section. http://www.nytimes.com/2008/02/01/business/worldbusiness/01fund.html?_r=1&oref=slogin (accessed May 6, 2008.)

[22] Edwin M. Truman, "Sovereign Wealth Fund Acquisitions and other Foreign Government Investment In the United States." Testimony be fore U.S. Senate, Committee on Banking, Housing, and Urban Affairs. November 14, 2007.

The Line That Cripples Society: Educated vs. Uneducated

Matthew Wilson

MEASURING A PERSON'S EDUCATION has become a general measuring tool for societal class. While basic education is being required up to a certain age, the economical world is now requiring at least a minimum of a high school diploma for most jobs. Yet, if these systems are in place, why is it that there are still so many Americans who are considered to be uneducated? In his essay, "Learning in the Key of Life," Jon Spayde writes, "There is no divide in American life that hurts more than the one between those we consider well educated and those who are poorly or inadequately schooled" (66).

The best point that Spayde makes is found in his opening remarks:

> What does it mean—and more important, what *should* it mean—to be educated? This is a surprisingly tricky two sided question. Masquerading as simple problem solving, it raises a whole laundry list of philosophical conundrums: What sort of society do we want? What is the nature of humankind? How do we learn best? And— most challenging of all—what is the Good? Talking about the meaning of education inevitably leads to the question of what a culture considers most important. (64)

Spayde is correct on several accounts by this series of questions. First, asking what it should mean to be educated. It has become in society that this question is answered by diplomas and degrees from respected educational institutions; one of the most respected higher education institutions in society today is Harvard University. Spayde quotes Henry David Thoreau who states, "I am self educated; that is, I attended Harvard College," Spayde adds, "indeed Harvard in the

73

early 19th century excelled mainly in the extent and violence of its food fights" (66). Now, Harvard is one of the nation's most highly respected universities for academics, but has street smart education mixed into its history.

How does one define a person as being well educated? Is being well educated judged by grades through the course of an academic career? Perhaps instead of focusing on academic test scores, more attention should be paid to life experiences. But in our current society, the level of education is only determined by letters printed on a card and are determined by someone who is thought to be well versed and highly educated on the subject. The fact is that as complex beings our incredibly complex brains differ greatly enough between people that there cannot truly be a standard set to test intelligence. Rather such standardized testing tests nothing more than our academic book smarts. A person whose mind fails to function fully is automatically deemed unintelligent, when they can be fully capable of leading normal and active lives. The only difference between the so called unintelligent and the intelligent is that they are not considered to have the ability to perform well when being addressed with questions found on standardized tests. Because of similar lines of thought, standardized testing is not the most effective, and the ever evolving world has tried to solve the problem by means of technology. By requiring employees to learn basic computer skills, one has now forced education upon another, instead of encouraging, and inspiring that person to learn on their own ambition.

Conversely, we have those who have been deemed as being less unintelligent. And by the scores of a standardized, timed test perhaps they cannot perform in a manner such as answering text book questions, but skilled labor and most employment skills come from experience and seizing opportunity, not from anything that can be received from a book. Likewise, most "unintelligent" are more commonly incredible geniuses when it comes to the theory of street smarts. In this case, a person has decided to achieve their success through knowledge by living the experiences of the real world. The smartest person may be able to find the answer to long drawn out textbook questions, but the simple fact is that the one with less intelligence, but greater life knowledge, is more likely to succeed on a long term scale than a person whose life is invested in memorizing books.

Now, the best situation between the two is obviously some middle ground. Where a person, has the ability to read and understand reading well, and at the same time has the abilities of common sense, and general knowledge received by day to day life. In corporate America, intelligence is a very important factor, but in order to rise through the levels of business one must possess the street smarts with which to swoon the people who make the top level decisions. They must also be able to establish and maintain a positive persona. Furthermore, to be successful in corporate business, it merely helps to be "educated," but through the proper training and the willingness to sacrifice the good of others, one can easily make his or her way through the ranks of corporate America.

The difference between being educated or uneducated cannot be determined by standardized testing or by the job or career path that person chooses. Education is, then, determined by a person's functionality. It is the fine line determined by those that consider themselves "educated" that metaphysically disables society, and it keeps us from living in a harmonious environment. By judging everyone from this line as being either educated or uneducated, we lose focus on whether or not we are in fact educated, and whether or not that education is strictly book education, street education, or a combination of the two. Until the time when we stop judging people based on education and give them the equal opportunity that is stressed in our society that allows them the chance to perform and succeed, we will not make any progress. Instead, we are simply disqualifying a person who is deemed uneducated from being able to succeed in life.

Work Cited

Spayde, Jon. "Learning in the Key of Life." *The Presence of Others*. 4th ed. Eds. Andrea A. Lunsford and John J. Ruszkiewicz. Boston: Bedford/St. Martin's, 2004. 64–69.

From the Rack to the Classroom

Howard Simmons

THE FIRST COMIC BOOK I REMEMBER reading (at least in any detail) was a three part series entitled *The Many Deaths of Batman*. I was in the fourth grade of elementary school and Tim Burton's film *Batman* had recently been released—much to the delight of ten year old boys everywhere. The movie and its brooding hero sent me giddily to the nearest comic book rack, which was haphazardly placed at the back of the magazine aisle of my hometown's grocery store.

Throughout most of junior high school years and on into the first year of high school, I read happily and greedily page upon page of panels: some stories told gaudily and brightly colored, others black and white and heavy with atmosphere.

As I entered high school and began to consider myself an adult, I came to see comics as something childish and a source of embarrassment. A staple of science fiction geeks, comics would only hinder my pursuit of acceptance among my peers and impede my growth into maturity. And, like others who relegate childhood pleasures to the stable of memories in order to pursue adulthood, I eventually placed all my comics in a box and pushed them to the back of the closet. Novels became my means of escape and recreation.

It wasn't until I had safely entered my twenties that I rediscovered my love for comics and realized they could offer more than mesmerizing stories of vengeance seeking men clad in spandex. I had picked up a copy of artist Daniel Clowes's *David Boring*, a murder mystery set on an island after the world may have come to an end.

As comic books have developed, beginning with their creation and booming popularity during World War II to the current myriad graphic novels in circulation today, they have steadily, but not without a fight, begun to build a reputation as more than childish recreation. Works such as Art Spiegelman's *Mause*, Will Eisner's *A Contract with God* (which Eisner himself proclaimed as the first graphic novel), and Alan Moore's *The Watchmen* have pushed the reader's knowledge of what a comic can be. Their topics range from superheroes to memoirs. They can be written for children—*Casper the Friendly Ghost*—or strictly for adults: Frank Miller's graphically violent and sexual *Sin City*.

The acceptance of comics and graphic novels—which consist of lengthier pieces of work or a collection of smaller vignettes that form a cohesive narrative when grouped together in panel by panel overlay—as a valid form of creative expression and high art has been more readily granted in the art community. Renee French, an artist whose work is featured primarily in comic format, has received praise as well as the chance to exhibit her artwork in museums such as the Swiss Institute in New York City. The embracement of the art community is more forthcoming to different forms of expression, while it is harder to gain in the literary community, often viewed as stodgy and elitist.

As graphic novels have gained in popularity and acceptance, the literary and education communities have come to see some worth in the form, primarily as a tool for education and an introduction to other, so called *higher* literary devices. Rich Shea, writing for *Teacher Magazine*, points out that many educators nationwide are using comic books as literacy tools. Graphic novels and comic books have proven an effective way to capture the attention of students who may be less than interested in reading. However, the use of graphic novels as a "stepping stone" also implies that it is still a less respected form. The graphic novel continues to waver on unsteady literary ground.

There is some debate about the artistic medium under which comic books should be classed. Undoubtedly, it is a primarily visual form, structured much like a film: readers move from one panel to the next, their eyes focusing first on the art then drifting to the written words comprising the character's dialogue, inner thoughts, or separate narrative voice. The minimal space given to the written word often demands conciseness of language and a skillful command of conveying briefly all that the writer intends or needs to say. When written effectively, language can heighten, sustain, or illuminate subtle emotions or offer a narrative structure to guide the artist in what he or she is trying to convey.

Some might argue that the very fact that so much importance is placed on the visual aspect of the graphic novel can't support the theory that it is also literature. But I would argue that the very complexity denotes a new form of literature, one in which the marriage of visuals and linguistics add another piece to the artistic puzzle, further conveying the uniqueness of human existence. As time progresses, so do the ways in which generations express themselves.

Peter Schjeldahl writes for *The New Yorker* that "graphic novels—pumped up comics—are to many in their teens and twenties what poetry once was, before bare words lost their cachet." A recent advertisement for a local art show in the Springfield, Missouri, area claimed that words were no longer the medium in which ideas were conveyed. As the world becomes increasingly streamlined, the visual medium becomes the fastest way to receive information. The artist/author of the graphic novel, when at the height of talent, can often convey the complexity of human emotions with a single panel and a few carefully written words.

In the 1980s, comic book writer Alan Moore showed the world that comics, specifically the superhero genre, could offer a plethora of ideas. The story of *The Watchmen*, set in an alternate 1980s where the Cold War still rages, focuses on a group of retired crime fighters who are being murdered by a masked serial killer. Moore switches effectively between pages of written word and the comic format, able to link and thereby show the differences and similarities between two supposedly separate identities. The result is a gripping, surprisingly emotional story that focuses on the regrets, failures, and mundane lives of those who had given of themselves for a larger ideal. Moore has consistently defied expectations and refuses to allow himself to be marginalized. A smarter, less sensational provocateur than fellow artist Frank Miller, his works increase dialogue about the medium, further the exchange of ideas, and, above all, use the medium in a way which tells a story to the best of his ability.

With the theatrical release of Frank Miller's *Sin City* in 2004, the cult graphic novels of the same name suddenly received a glaring spotlight of attention from the media. Mimicking Miller's stark black and white pages punctured by splashes of bawdy colors, the movie was an unrelenting phantasmagoria of violence, hyper sexuality, and gore. It was a raging success. *Sin City's* neo noir stories illustrate perfectly the progression of a medium that was primarily seen as something for children and now places it firmly in adult territory. Its stories of prostitution, cannibalism, and mass murder are anything but child's fare.

Not all graphic novels are as sensational, however. Comic artists and writers such as Daniel Clowes, author of *Ghost World* and *Ice Haven*, and Chris Ware, author of *Jimmy Corrigan: The Smartest Boy in the World*, have garnered respect in both the art and literary community. *Ghost World*, the story of two girls who are in flux between high school and adulthood, is a strange, heart wrenching account of displacement to which most of its readers can relate. Clowes's work "plays crisp, bland cartooning, at times reminiscent of the old *Can You Draw This?* matchbook ads, against stealthily nuanced writing" (Schjeldahl, *New Yorker*). It is only because of Clowes' talent as a writer that Schjeldahl uses the term "stealthily nuanced." Clowes' ability as a writer helps the artwork take on an additional dimension and offers new wonders to the reader.

In 1992, Art Spiegelman won the Pulitzer Prize for his story, *Maus: A Survivor's Tale*. Drawing Jews as mice and Germans as cats, Spiegelman told the story of his father's internment in a concentration camp. His use of anthropomorphism allowed him to tell a terrible, horrifying story in a way that subdued the more exploitative elements and heightened the horror and emotional impact for the reader.

Because of the varying genres of graphic novels, their importance as artistic expression can often be overlooked. The graphic novel's relegation in scholars' minds as an effective tool for education, while valid, marginalizes its impact. There are critics who argue that most comics used in classrooms are either dumbed down or too inappropriate (Shea 16). This is not an entirely fair assessment, since it has been stated that graphic novels require more cognitive skills (Schwarz 262). As Schjeldahl writes, "Consuming them—toggling for hours between the incommensurable functions of reading and looking—is taxing" (162). Schejeldahl even states that reading comics demands and rewards mental flexibility and nervous stamina. He further supposes in his article that graphic novels have come of age. His view, while held by others, denotes a conception of the graphic novel and comic books in general as a passing movement, although others would argue that it is still progressing as a medium.

One could argue that as literature changes and adapts, so too will the graphic novel. The graphic novel should be viewed neither as a lesser literary genre nor as a mere tool to catch the interest of illiterate children, but rather as a different form of art—a marriage of artistic and literary capabilities. The graphic novel still offers a plethora of new ideas and visions that readers have yet to discover.

Works Cited

Clowes, Daniel. "Blue Italian Shit." *Caricature*. Seattle: Fantagraphic Books. 25–31.

——. *David Boring*. New York: Pantheon Books, 2000.

——. *Ghost World*. Seattle: Fantagraphic Books, 1998.

Eisner, Will. *A Contract With God*. New York: DC Comics.

Moore, Alan. *Watchmen*. New York: DC Comics, 1995.

Nadel, Dan. "The Dark Stuff." Print Mar/Apr 2006: 70–75.

Schwarz, Gretchen E. "Graphic Novels for Multiple Litera cies." *Journal of Adolescent and Adult Literacy* Nov. 2002: 262–65.

Schjeldahl, Peter. "Words and Picture: Graphic Novels Come of Age." *The New Yorker* 81 (2005): 162–68.

Second Baptist Church. Advertisement. *KY3*. Sept. 2006

Shea, Rich. "Comics in the Classroom." *Teacher Magazine* Oct. 2006: 16–17.

Spiegelman, Art. *Maus: A Survivor's Tale*. New York: Pan theon.

The Utilization of Obese Individuals in Pandemic Viral Prevention with an Emphasis on Avian Influenza

Heather Bingham

Introduction

IN ORDER TO OBTAIN USABLE MATERIAL for research of pandemic viral pathogens, researchers much isolate preserved tissue samples from the lungs of human victims of past pandemics that contain intact viral components for genetic sequencing. Geographic areas containing permafrost are typically targeted as permafrost prevents the biological process of decomposition of the corpse. However, researchers have often met with the challenge that extreme cold temperatures cause permanent damage to the viral components necessary for research. To efficiently obtain valid viral samples in an expeditious manner, researchers must narrow down the scope of the sample population and focus on *obese* corpses preserved within the permafrost. An obese corpse provides the necessary insulation to preserve lung tissues, but more importantly, it prevents the denaturation of the RNA and protein structures of the virus itself. By implementing a specific focus in the field of research, valuable resources of time, effort, and cost are significantly reduced. The information obtained can then be used in scientific analysis and medical applications toward current and future viral epidemics.

Background

THE 1918 SPANISH FLU PANDEMIC is used as the basis for research as it had the greatest impact on global human populations and preceded viral strains of all recent avian influenza outbreaks within the last century. Within a year of the Spanish flu outbreak, between twenty and fifty million people worldwide, one fifth of the global human population, had been killed.[1] In 1917, after the United States entered World War I, several army training camps were constructed. Camp Sherman, the third largest of these camps, was stationed in the small town of Chillicothe, Ohio, bringing with it the Spanish flu and resulting in an outbreak of the entire town, killing thousands. The local theatre, "The Majestic," was used as an emergency storage facility for bodies of the dead, which were piled like cordwood on the stage. Blood and body fluids ran out into the alley, which is known to this day as "Blood Alley."[2] The Spanish flu was unique from other viral outbreaks in several ways. People died very quickly from the virus, within two to three days of showing symptoms. The virus caused the victims' lungs to fill with blood and fluid, causing death by drowning. Additionally, victims tended to be young and healthy, unlike the victims of the majority of influenza outbreaks, which target the elderly and the very young individuals in a community. Table 1 exhibits the high mortality rate of young adults, peaking around the age of twenty five.

Obese Individual Key to Sequencing Hemagglutinin Gene of the 1918 Virus

GIVEN THE MASSIVE IMPACT the pandemic had on the globe, numerous researchers have attempted to research the viral components of the Spanish flu. In 1995, Jeffery Taubenberger,[4] a US virologist with the Armed Forces Institute of Pathology, decided to continue the work of previous researchers in finding and sequencing the remains of the Spanish flu of 1918. Despite access to the government warehouse remains of seventy seven soldiers who had died in the pandemic, Taubenberger's[4] team was only able to locate one victim with fragments of the 1918 influenza virus contained in the tissue of a single lung. The tissue belonged to an army private named Roscoe Vaughn, who had died at Camp Jackson in South Carolina. Using the application of primers and Polymerase Chain Reaction (PCR), the team used over half the tissue sample in sequencing only one gene of the virus. A simplified molecular model of the gene is depicted in Figure 2. Research was detained until Johan Hultin,[4] a pathologist who had tried to isolate the 1918 Spanish influenza virus from Alaskan victims buried in permafrost in 1951, offered Taubenberger[4] his assistance in returning to Alaska in search of more preserved victims for research. Through a fortunate coincidence, Hultin[4] unearthed the remains of an obese woman aged around thirty years. The insulation from her body fat had protected both of her lungs from decay. More importantly, the insulation from her fat had protected the protein and RNA components of the virus. This proved to be the key to completing the research, as it resulted in enough material to sequence the complete 1918 virus many times over.

There are some who may contend that exhuming the corpses of human victims from their graves is disrespectful and suggest that animals or some lesser being should be the subject of study of the influenza infection. This process may be ill mannered; it is, however, unavoidable in terms of preservation of future human life. The nature of a virus is to adapt itself to the cell functions of the species upon which it preys to ensure viable reproduction. A virus which originates within the body of one organism will undergo genetic mutations within the body of a different organism, which enable it to better function within the new environment. Because there are biological differences in composition and function between species, the reaction of the organism to the newly mutated viral form are specific to each species. The potential of the virus to mutate and move between species was, in fact, the basis for the pandemic outbreak in 1918. An image of the Spanish flu virus is portrayed in Figure 3. The virus is thought to have originated as an avian strain which mutated into a form adapted to humans. Thus, due to the specific nature of an influenza virus within a human, the only valid remaining element of the outbreak is contained within the lung tissues of human victims. In addition to the scientific validity of this process, the utmost respect is used in exhuming bodies from grave sites. During both of his missions, Hultin[4] took great care in explaining the purpose of his research to the people of the village in Brevig, Alaska and obtained permission to dig in the grave site of the victims. Special acknowledgement is also given to the people of Brevig, Alaska in scientific journals which report on the progress of the influenza research.

Preserved Resources of Time and Cost

THE VAST PLANE OF INFORMATION regarding an influenza infection and its impact on the human species requires researchers to narrow their field of research. By designating obese individuals within permafrost as the objective in the search for possible intact viral samples, ample expenses of time and cost are spared. When Johan Hultin[4] made his first mission to Brevig, Alaska in 1951, he unearthed several bodies of victims from the 1918 influenza virus but failed to find any valid viral material. The viral components contained within the victims' bodies had been subjected to biological decay during the brief periods of thaw. It was forty six years later before Hultin returned to the Brevig grave site and was fortunate enough to unearth the body of an obese female. As previously mentioned, the adipose cells of her body had insulated the viral RNA and protein components necessary for genetic sequencing. Had researchers known the value of searching for obese individuals at the onset of research, half a century worth of time would have been restored to the viral research. During the period of time that research was delayed due to lack of available material, 1951–1997, millions of human lives were lost to avian viral pandemics. In 1957–1958 an Asian flu arose from fowl, causing seventy thousand deaths in the United States and two million deaths world wide.[6] In 1968–1969, the "Hong Kong flu" arose from fowl, resulting in thirty four thousand more deaths in the United States.[5] In addition to reducing time spent on unproductive research, having a specific focus to guide the onset of research is highly valuable in obtaining grants, intramural funds, and other financial means of support for the research. A focus driven project with lowered costs will present itself as a much more credible project to financial creditors.

Critics may claim that by isolating the research sample to a single type of individual, results may become biased. However, under the unique conditions of past viral pandemics, there is a very specific set of limitations placed on material for research. The two most viable sources of possible research material are restricted to bodies preserved by government disease control agencies and those found preserved in nature. Research under natural conditions is limited to corpses preserved within geographic areas containing permafrost, which introduces the additional requirement of insulation to protect the viral components. Given the uncontrollable factors of biological decomposition and denaturation under natural conditions, the additional factor of body insulation is necessary to obtain any type of intact viral material for research.

Prevention of Future Pandemics

THE THREE PRIMARY STRATEGIES for controlling influenza outbreaks are surveillance, vaccination, and treatment.

Viral pandemics are most threatening among populations of humans who have no immunity to the virus. The best method of preparedness against future avian viral pandemics is to study the composition of related viral species of past pandemics and use the information to develop vaccinations and antiviral drugs. Viral pandemics among humans have been caused by three subtypes of the influenza A virus: H1N1, H2N2, and H3N2.[6] The Spanish flu pandemic of 1918 was caused by the H1N1 subtype. In the Asian influenza pandemic of 1957, the H2N2 virus appeared. The influenza pandemic of 1968 started in Hong Kong and was caused by an H3N2 virus.[6] Aquatic birds are the reservoir for all known subtypes of influenza A viruses and as such are the source from which pandemic influenza viruses arise. As evidenced by the past three pandemics, the influenza A virus continues to evolve into different forms which infect humans. The virus can either pass directly from birds to humans or be introduced into the human population after reassortment with circulating human influenza A viruses. Without the information obtained by sequencing the genome of the Spanish flu, the human species would have no defense against any subset of avian flu. Methods, such as purpose driven searches of obese victims of past pandemics preserved in permafrost, must continually be developed in order to obtain the crucial information needed to design medical prevention against the deadly effects of the virus.

Despite the massive impact of the previous pandemics on the global human population, a large majority of modern day individuals remain skeptical of future pandemics becoming reality. This is likely attributed to false predictions of catastrophic pandemics from viruses such as the swine flu scare of 1976, the Russian flu scare of 1977, the avian A/ H5N1 flu in 1997, and most recently, SARS in 2002.[7] Despite the prevention of pandemics from the past several viral scares, experts maintain that mutated forms of an existing avian virus could evolve and sweep populations with no immunity. All influenza A viruses are presumed to have pandemic potential and current vaccine development activities are largely focused on viruses of this subtype. A reemergence of the highly pathogenic avian A/H5N1 virus in Asia has raised concerns of a potential pandemic, resulting in an augmented level of preparedness for such an event. A pandemic preparedness plan for the United States was published in November 2005.[6] Table 2 shows the global growth rate of the H5N1 virus from 2004 to 2006.

Conclusion

GIVEN THE REALITY OF AVIAN INFLUENZA threat on present and future human populations, the method of searching out naturally preserved bodies of obese individuals from previous avian flu pandemics is a crucial technique that must be applied to scientific research. Through establishment of a specific focus in sampling, unnecessary field and research time expenses are eliminated, cost is reduced, and scientific and medical discoveries are given the potential for expedited results. As viruses continue to adapt and evolve, the field of scientific research must do the same. The best defense against the offensive habits of the avian influenza virus is preparedness and the essential level of preparedness needed for the preservation of human life can only be achieved as a product of viable research material.

References

1. Is It Possible That the Spanish Flu Can "Survive" in Permafrost? [Internet]. [cited 2008 Apr 27]. Available from: http://www.ontariogenomics.ca/education/pdfs/s1e12.pdf

2. Billings M. The Influenza Pandemic of 1918 [Internet]; 2007 June [cited 2008 Apr 12]. Available from: http://virus.stanford.edu/uda/#top

3. Camp Sherman [Internet]. [place unknown]: [cited 2008 Apr 12]. Available from: http://www.nps.gov/archive/hocu/html/sherman.html

4. Wikipedia contributors. Jeffery Taubenberger [Internet]. Wikipedia, The Free Encyclopedia; 2008 Mar 7, 21:14 UTC [cited 2008 Apr 11]. Available from: http://en.wikipedia.org/w/index.php?title=Jeffery_Taubenberger&oldid=196615132

5. Richards D, M.D. Nobel Laureate in Medicine, 1956. [Internet]. [cited 2008 Apr 28]. Available from: http://www.columbia.edu/itc/hs/medical/pathophys/pulmonary/2006/pulm012506_Schluger01BW.pdf

6. Rotondo RD. Preparing for the Next Pandemic [Internet]. Mediscovery, Inc. 2007. [cited 2008 Apr 11]. Available from: http://www.mediscovery.com/influenza.html

7. Lovgren S. Is Asian Bird Flu the Next Pandemic? National Geographic News. 2004 Dec [cited 2008 April 11]. Available from: http://news.nationalgeographic.com/news/2004/12/1207_041207_birdflu.html

8. Reid AH, Fanning TG, Hultin JV, Taubenberger JK. Origin and evolution of the 1918 "Spanish" influenza virus hemagglutinin gene. Proc. Natl. Acad. Sci. USA. 1999 Feb: 1651–1656.

Organic Foods: Should We Abandon or Embrace Them?

Julie Whitson

Introduction

RECENTLY, PEOPLE HAVE THROWN the debate about organic foods into the limelight. Some supporters say that organic food drastically reduces environmental problems, supports a good cause, and that the difference in taste and nutrients seems obvious. Opponents claim that the entire organic movement poses a threat to productivity and efficiency in the agricultural market. So the question remains: Should we go with what we know and currently do, or should we aim to support a grassroots movement that could deliver us from environmental consequences? Organic food may not possess every positive quality that its supporters say it does, but the organic foods movement supports good natured goals, such as limiting farm workers' exposure to harmful pesticides, reducing environmental consequences, and lessening animal exposure to pesticides and antibiotics.

Review 1

IN THE ARTICLE "Rediscovering the Human Biosphere" published in Consumer Health Newsletter, David Suzuki (2005) describes his opinions about the organic movement from the perspective of a genetic scientist. He asserts that even if we cannot foresee the potential problems that new technology will present years down the road, we should at least understand that the water we drink, the air we breathe, and the land on which we live and grow our food will always play a vital role in our survival. In the 1930s, scientists unleashed a chemical named Dichloro Diphenyl

Trichloroethane (DDT) that targeted pesky bugs like mosquitoes. Even though the scientific community had conducted many experiments on how well it could perform, the article reminds readers of Rachel Carson's book Silent Spring, which presented evidence that DDT affected organisms other than insects, like fish, birds, and ultimately human beings (p. 2).

When technology led to the discovery of chlorofluorocarbons (CFCs) to use as filler in aerosol cans, Suzuki (2005) explains how a similar situation ensued. CFCs did not react with active ingredients in the cans they filled; however, once consumers deposited them into the air, they floated into the upper portion of our atmosphere and their interaction with ultra violet rays produced free floating atoms that literally ate away at the ozone layer. Only until several million pounds of CFCs had accumulated did we realize a problem existed.

Review 2

DDT AND CFCs DO NOT POSE the only problems to our environment. Tina Adler (2002) indicates in the article "Harmful Farming," published in Environmental Health Perspectives, that agricultural practices today not only add pollutants and other harmful items to our environment, but they also shut down local farm economies and waste natural resources, like fossil fuels, topsoil, and water. The agriculture industry's widespread use of pesticides since the 1950s leaves some people skeptical as to whether or not the sheer volume of pesticides farmers use to get the job done today truly helps the growing of crops. According to Adler (2002), "Crops absorb only one third to one half of fertilizer applications, and less than one percent of applied pesticide reaches the target pests" (p. 256). Runoff carries the unused pesticides to area waterways, accounting for 70% of the river and stream pollution in the United States.

As decades ago with DDT and other pesticides currently used, Adler (2002) states that as of 1990, pesticides have caused 500 species to become immune to the strains of pesticides that are used today (p. 256). Unfortunately for the agriculture industry, it is not only pesticide overuse that creates problems; according to Adler (2002), "Seventy percent of antibiotics produced in the United States are fed to healthy animals as growth promoters" (256). The staggering amount of antibiotics fed to animals to prevent infection contributes to the worldwide problem of antibiotic resistance. In the same fashion that bugs mutate to overcome the latest poisons meant to kill them, bacteria worldwide have started to mutate to get around the effects that antibiotics used to have on them. By overexposing bacteria to antibiotics, we give bacteria more opportunities to mutate into something that can resist our current antibiotics.

Review 3

THE OVERALL DIFFERENCE IN TASTE and nutrients in organic food is not always evident, but Marion Nestle (2005) agrees with Adler (2002) in the article "In Praise of the Organic Environment" published in Global Agenda that the difference between organic foods and regularly grown foods may not seem overwhelming, but one can find the difference in what organic foods do for the environment. Since 1990, sales each year have gone up by about 20 percent, and in 2004 organic foods pulled in roughly 20 billion dollars (p. 218). This tells us that in some way organic foods have succeeded in making their mark. People who oppose organic foods say that no difference exists between organic and regular foods except the price; however, Nestle (2005) reveals just what it takes for foods to earn an organic certification:

> [The producers] did not use any synthetic pesticides, herbicides, or fertilizers to grow crops or feed for animals; they did not use crops of feed that had been genetically

93

modified, fertilized with sewage sludge or irradiated; they did not feed animals the by products of other animals; . . . and they were inspected to make sure they followed the rules in letter . . . (p. 218).

When comparing organic and regular foods, one will notice the difference in price first and foremost. Obtaining USDA organic certification in the United States is still not easy. The fee for certification remains costly, most organic farms maintain a higher and fairer working wage, organic farms operate on a smaller scale in order to tend to agriculture as they see fit, and organic farms do not receive government subsidies like other farmers in the agriculture industry. Some opponents of organic foods question the productivity factor on an organic farm; however, research conducted over a period of years shows that "farmers who converted from conventional to organic methods experienced small declines in yields, but these losses were offset by lower fuel costs and better conserved soils" (Nestle, 2005, p. 219). Both of these benefits to organic farmers show direct benefits to the environment.

Many critics also question the safety of some organic methods, such as using manure. Even the manure must meet a certification standard to ensure that the food gets the necessary nutrients without the harmful microbes (2% fecal contaminants on traditionally grown, 4% on certified organic, and 11% on produce said to be organic, but not certified) (Nestle, 2005, p. 219). In short, organic foods' "true value comes from what they do for farm workers in lower pesticide exposure, for soils in enrichment and conservation, for water supplies in less fertilizer runoff . . . for fish in protection against contamination with organic hydrocarbons, and for other such environmental factors" (Nestle, 2005, p. 219).

Discussion

THE ORGANIC MOVEMENT PROVIDES a solution to the problems we face dealing with pesticides and the environment. Suzuki (2005) reminds us that we have obviously had problems in the past with chemicals like DDT and CFCs affecting the environment, but only when people spotted the damage did we do something about it. As Hyla Cass (2006) says in her article titled "Environmental Toxin Imbalances" about a recent British study, "The most alarming finding was that 99 percent of those tested had residues of the pesticide DDT in their blood, despite the fact that it had been banned decades ago" (p. 26). The pesticide worked its way up the food chain and effected many aspects of the environment. Even though the government eventually banned DDT, the original pest insects have still developed biological adaptations to this pesticide just as they do to similar pesticides used today.

The United States currently outdoes all other countries in their pesticide usage according to an article in Essence, accounting for half of the worldwide usage—two billion pounds a year (Wiltz, 1994, p.24). However, this sheer amount of pesticide usage does not just come from the large agricultural base in our economy. Applying pesticides as much as we do illustrates the problems we face with bugs becoming resistant to the chemicals we currently overuse.

When arguing for organic foods, some activists raise the supposed notion that organic food tastes better and has more nutrients. Scientists cannot quantify these opinions and only found a slightly elevated level of nutrients in certain organic foods. As a personal health benefit, organic foods do not offer a distinct advantage. However, by supporting the organic food movement, one can also make a statement about environmental factors, such as using pesticides, protecting wildlife from groundwater runoff and contamination, and helping to lessen soil erosion. By buying organic foods, one can also help small, local farms survive and stop farm workers' exposure to harmful pesticides, which have been proven to cause certain types of cancer and endocrine damage in the human body. These chemicals affect anyone, especially children, who come in contact with them before they shower and change clothes. The sheer amount of pesticides the United States currently uses (50% of world expenditure) could also point to our quick fix solution to bugs' biological adaptation to current pesticides.

Conclusion

THE ARGUMENTS SURROUNDING THIS TOPIC seem slanted from both perspectives, but this movement at least supports good natured goals, such as limiting farm workers' exposure to harmful pesticides, limiting environmental consequences, and lessening animal exposure to pesticides and antibiotics. The organic movement poses a solution to the problems that surround the overuse of pesticides and fertilizers before we reach a point in which we must take drastic measures to repair the damage that we have already done. The environmental problems caused by pesticides have not yet reached a peak in which activism has become necessary to avoid permanent damage. The organic foods movement seems so controversial because no one has proven a direct correlation with irreversible damage and the need to act now. Even if we cannot verify direct personal benefits from organic food, remember that purchasing organic food will make a statement about an issue that concerns all aspects of the environment.

References

Adler, T (2002). Harmful farming. *Environmental Health Perspectives*, 110 (5), p. 256. Retrieved March 14, 2007, from Academic Search Premier database.

Cass, H (2006). Environmental toxin imbalances. *Total Health*, 28 (1), p. 26–30. Retrieved March 11, 2007, from Alt Health Watch database.

Nestle, M (2005). In praise of the organic environment. *Global Agenda*, 3, p. 218–19. Retrieved March 11, 2007, from Academic Search Premier database.

Suzuki, D (2005). Rediscovering the human place in the biosphere. *Consumer Health Newsletter*, 28 (2), p. 2–4. Retrieved March 11, 2007, from Alt Health Watch data base.

Wiltz, T (1994). Bugging out. *Essence*, 25 (2), p. 24. Re trieved March 14, 2007, from Academic Search Premier database.

Ein Finsteres Vermächtnis: *The Connection Between 19ᵗʰ Century Colonialism and the Nazi Regime*

Sean A. Wempe

Introduction: The Lost Pages of History

TYPICALLY, WHEN AN ANALYSIS of the Colonial Era and its impact is made, the examples that are focused on are those of British and French colonialism. This is understandable, since they were the power players who formed empires and commonwealths that endured for generation after generation, but there were others on the colonial scene that tend to be forgotten, particularly the relatively short appearance of Germany on the stage of colonial endeavors. Historians and laity alike often fall into the mental trap of regarding 19ᵗʰ century German colonialism as a failure, a mere outcropping of Bismarckian Imperialism that was ill fated and short lived. Such a view, however, ignores the great impact that German colonialism had, not only in shaping the history of those continents and islands that witnessed its colonial presence, but also on the German nation itself. As a result, there is simply not enough analysis of this topic that would seem to have much relevance to any complete understanding of Germany's history. Luckily, some scholars are now beginning to explore this previously neglected period in Germany's past and are finding more and more connections between this era and the mentalities and policies of later portions of German history and Western civilization as a whole. Germany's brief ascendancy during the colonial period had a profound impact not only on its colonies, but also Germany itself, altering the nation's view of itself and its relation to others, creating a German "colonial mentality" that was to have notable influence during the Nazi regime.

Ein Riesiges Reich: The Extent of Germany's Original Colonial Empire

IN ORDER TO FULLY UNDERSTAND the level of an impact colonialism had on Germany's sense of identity, one must first understand how deeply it became involved in building a Kolonialreich in its brief interlude in this era of world history. Though many don't know it, from 1881, when Bismarck gave into interest groups pressuring for colonies, to 1914, when the nation lost them to the Allies, Germany constructed and controlled the third largest colonial empire in the world, bested only by England and France. This empire was extremely diversified, with the Germans holding sway over numerous islands in the Pacific, as well as controlling a large section of Africa, including modern day Namibia, Togo, the Cameroons, and Tanzania, that extended over a 900,000 square mile portion of the globe, "four times the area of the [European] Reich." Such a large sphere of influence certainly exemplified Bismarck's concept of the Balance of Power between the great nations of Europe, giving Germany relatively equal political clout with the giants of England and France.

The Germans were also not passive landlords of their colonies. They invested heavily, morally, and monetarily, into what they viewed as their portion of "The White Man's Burden" to civilize the more primitive nations of the world, and were praised by their colonial contemporaries. And, in fact, they did bring many positives to the world colonial stage. They introduced Western technology and philosophies to Africa, including the two sided sword of ethnography, constructed dock yards and roads, and laid some 4,500 kilometers of railway track to facilitate industry and transport within their colonies. In terms of what they brought back to Europe from their colonies, the Germans were pioneers in the study of African languages, and also produced African scholars, such as Anton Wilhelm Amo, who enriched European philosophy by offering different perspectives. Germany was certainly becoming a colonial powerhouse, investing more, and, though entering late to the colonial scene, quickly outstripping its contemporaries in development and management of its colonies.

Der Kolonialgeist: Germany's Colonial Mindset

GIVEN HOW HEAVILY Germany invested in its colonies, and as dependent as it became on the possession of such colonies for national grandeur mimicking the other great nations of Europe, it is no wonder that the German population felt a profound sense of loss, materially and ideologically, when the Allies stripped it of its satellites at the end of the First World War. From this loss and humiliation, a sentiment of desire to return to colonial grandeur arose, adding to the formation of Germany's dangerous preoccupation with restitution for the injustices that had been inflicted on it by the Allies.

As early as 1918, special interest groups, such as the Reichsbund der Kolonialdeutschen (RBKD) and the extremely influential Deutsche Kolonialgesellschaft (DKG), were formed by those Germans who had lost homes, property, or positions of power through the loss of the colonies. These numerous "colonial clubs" that arose following the stripping of Germany's colonies after the First World War were composed of elite individuals of a very conservative mentality and constituted only a small fraction of the society, but had a large political voice and represented Germany's desire to return to glory. By May of 1930, a conference of former colonial ministers was agitating the Weimar Republic to regain Germany's colonies with a list of seven guidelines, outlining such expectations as equal rights for Germans everywhere, protection of the German culture abroad, an understanding worldwide that some of Germany's colonies were not ready to be independent (coupled with a desire to see increased efforts and propaganda for the German government to acquire mandates), and, most importantly, a renunciation of the "Colonial Guilt Lie," a not wholly unjustified statement made by the Allies that the Germans had been poor colonial administrators who had violently abused their colonial subjects.

Dr. Heinrich Schnee, former governor of German East Africa (Tanganyika—modern day Tanzania), was not only at the head of the DKG and organizer of the conference of former ministers in 1930, but was also the most vehement advocate on the world stage for the return of Germany's former colonies. In 1926, Dr. Schnee wrote and published a protest called German Colonization: Past and Future: The Truth About the German Colonies, denouncing the "Colonial Guilt Lie" that he called a myth cooked up by the Allies to justify their control of Germany's former mandates. In his argument throughout the book, he tries to refute this sentiment of Germany's "colonial guilt" by outlining his view of German administration in the colonies, the praise it received from other imperial nations when it entered the colonial arena, and the sentiments of the natives to the Germans as opposed to those nations who held those nations subsequently as mandates and protectorates. Schnee also used Wilson's Fourteen Points to defend heavily the right of Germany to keep its colonies, citing Point Five as his main argument: both Germany and its colonies were denied the right of self determination by such actions, and the Allies acted selfishly in their own interests, in essence sentencing Germany and its colonies to ruin and thus should be responsible for rectifying this action by restoring Germany to its former glory.

Schnee's work was obviously biased, but it well portrayed the sentiments and national attachments that a significant portion of the German population felt towards their colonies at the time and signifies the level of impact the loss of those colonies had on Germany economically and emotionally. This sentiment did not fall on deaf ears. Though it at first seemed focused on solely domestic and continental affairs, the Nazi party soon made appeals to this very affluent portion of the population by alluding to the possibility of reestablishing Germany's overseas empire. Political alliances were formed, and colonialism once again became a matter of importance to the German government once the Nazi regime firmly entrenched itself.

Ein Finsteres Vermächtnis: The Dark Legacy Reapplied by the Nazi Regime

THE NAZIS FOUND THIS SENSE of injustice and the desire for restitution of the colonies a useful tool in their rise to power and expansion across Europe and North Africa, but that wasn't all that they tapped into from the colonial psyche. Hitler and his henchmen seem to have employed two much older, and far more horrible, elements of early German Colonialism to justify their actions at home and abroad—the concept of the "White Man's Burden" to civilize the world, and the atrocious tradition of mass genocide as a method to gain and maintain control of an area.

The Nazi party perpetuated the colonial concept of the "White Man's Burden," but did so in a way far removed from what the original colonizing powers had. While former colonial powers, including Germany, had viewed the continents of Africa, Asia, and America as uncivilized and in need of a sort of paternal aide and development, Nazi Germany applied this concept to their European neighbors: "For the Nazis, the acquisition of colonies outside of Europe took a backseat to [continental] expansion" though they still needed to appease colonial tendencies and desire for economic gain. Upon an examination of the Nazi occupational policy and Aryanism, one can see that the entire campaign into

Eastern Europe by the Nazis, on the grounds of Lebensraum and the sentiment that the Slavic nationalities were an inferior people, was more than just an occupation of foreign territory during a war, but was actually an application of formal colonialism directed against fellow Europeans. The Nazis built cities and railways while blatantly "disregarding indigenous settlements and economic structures" in regions that they viewed as undeveloped tabulae rasae, moving in settlers and establishing new industries to replace "chaos" with "order."

However, a far more terrible legacy was carried on by the Nazis, not only in the newly conquered territories but also within the German state itself—mass extermination of entire groups, based on ethnicity, deemed a threat to the government's authority. In Nazi Germany, "the rise of Eugenics and a politics of dissimilation between Germans and those not considered German went hand in hand with increasing interconnections of metropole and colony. Germans linked belonging to the German nation with whiteness," continuing a viewpoint that had been true of German colonialists in Africa and Asia. This view of other races as inferior had, in the past, justified the mass extermination of numerous African tribes when they rebelled against colonial authority. The Herero and Nama of modern day Namibia, the Abo and Bakoko of the Cameroons, the Konkomba of Togo, and most violently, the 250,000 to 300,000 Massai who were killed in the Maji Maji rebellion of 1905 in Tanganyika are examples of tribes who were subjected to this horrible fate by the German colonial powers. Some scholars argue that the Holocaust against the Jews and other "undesirables" by the Nazis was actually the final product of years of experimentation in genocide that had taken place in the colonies in Africa, asserting that those horrific "exterminatory wars" made the atrocities of the Nazi regime easier for the German populace to stomach, essentially normalizing mass extermination. Once a group, such as the

Jews or Slavs, had been labeled inferior, it seems natural that the same desensitized view that was directed against rebellious Africans would apply, the cries of those groups who were used as a scapegoat by the Nazis going unheard as they suffered the implementation of the "Final Solution" that had been used time and time before.

Conclusion: Research the Past to Understand the Present and to Possibly Foresee the Future

MORE SCHOLARSHIP MUST BE DONE on Germany's colonial period. Though Germany's ascendancy during the colonial period was brief, it affected how Germany viewed itself and had a profound impact on those nations it had once ruled, this "colonial mentality" horribly manifested during the Nazi regime. Further study of Bismarkian and Wilhelmine colonialism may not only shed light on this terrible time period of Germany's history, but may also prove an invaluable asset in understanding Cold War and contemporary Germany as well. With Germany's growth as a political and economic rather than military dominance in the European Union, as well as its more recent pushes to gain veto authority in the United Nations, delving into the treasure trove of this now peaceful nation's colonial history would seem a worthwhile endeavor in order to better understand the force that might once again rise as one of the strongest powers in the world.

Bibliography

Blackshire Belay, Carol Aisha. "German Imperialism in Africa: The Distorted Images of Cameroon, Namibia, Tanzania, and Togo." *Journal of Black Studies* 23, no. 2 (1992): 235–46. http://links.jstor.org (13 October 2006).

Poiger, Uta G. "Imperialism and Empire in Twentieth Cen tury Germany." *History and Memory* 17, no. 1/2 (2005): 117–43. http://search.ebscohost.com (22 September 2006).

Schmokel, Wolfe W. *Dream of Empire: German Colonialism, 1919–1945*. London: Yale, 1964.1–45.

Schnee, Heinrich. *German Colonization Past and Future: The Truth About the German Colonies*. London: George Allen & Unwin, 1926.

Zimmerer, Jürgen. "The birth of the Ostland out of the spirit of colonialism: a postcolonial perspective on the Nazi policy of conquest and extermination." *Patterns of Prejudice* 39, no. 2 (2005): 197–219. http://search.ebsco host.com (22 September 2006).

Chapter Three:

Rhetorical Analyses

Censoring the Magic

Allison Miller

IN THE FEBRUARY 2008 ISSUE of *Teen Ink*, a national teen magazine devoted entirely to teenage writing, writer Jared Misner from Clearwater, Florida, published a piece titled "The Silenced Sorcerer." This article discussed censorship of books and other materials and how allowing such a practice to exist violates Americans' freedoms. Specifically, he addressed how this action has been aimed at the tremendously popular *Harry Potter* series. Obviously a Potter fan, Misner attempts to sway readers to view censorship as a negative act that rarely accomplishes what it sets out to do.

Jared Misner begins his article by defining the word "censorship." According to the American Library Association, it is the "Suppression of ideas and information that certain persons [. . .] find objectionable or dangerous" (Misner). The rest of Misner's introduction questions the practice of censorship by asking who has the authority to decide what should be censored and also who is being protected by allowing it to happen.

The next section of Misner's piece includes several different appeals to help sway readers to his way of thinking. First of all, he uses logos, or facts and reason, when he reminds his readers that under the First Amendment, Americans are guaranteed their freedom of the press. He then asserts that, though Americans should be able to read whatever they desire, it is not the case. Censorship is very common, even in children's literature. Misner states, "After growing concerns about the witchcraft, 'dark images,' and violence in the *Harry Potter* books, the series topped the list of frequently banned books in America from 1999–2001" (Misner).

At this point in the article the author begins asking deep rhetorical questions once more, which serve as an effective technique to sway the reader into seeing the argument the way Misner wants him or her to see it. He asks, "Does a school have the authority to restrict students' access to information?" And also, "Aren't schools designed to promote diversity of knowledge and an education free of political opinions and propaganda?" (Misner). By questioning in such a way, Misner is employing a second rhetorical strategy: This time he uses pathos or emotional appeals. He is successful in making us feel emotional regarding our children's right to a proper, nonrestrictive education.

Misner then brings up two notable Supreme Court cases, *Hazelwood School District v. Kuhlmeier* and *Right to Read Defense Committee of Chelsea v. School Committee of the City of Chelsea*, that debate the issue of censoring reading material for school age children. He notes that the verdicts of the two cases disagree with one another. The first one ruled that principals have the authority to censor reading material that is deemed inappropriate. However, at the time of its verdict, Justice William Brennan disagreed, "This ruling violates the First Amendment's prohibitions against censorship of the press. Limiting expression limits education and strangles the mind." The other case found that, "[a] school should be a readily accessible warehouse of ideas that are not only presenting one side of an idea, but all" (Misner). This ruling, Misner informs readers, contradicts the other case and means that school libraries are not permitted to exclude certain books from their shelves. By bringing up these two cases, Misner is again using logos as he is citing specific instances and facts to back up his argument. By continually backing up his claims, he also appears more trustworthy to readers, bolstering his ethos as a credible writer.

Next, the author begins to discuss *Harry Potter* and those in opposition to the series. He notes that many Christian parents object when the books are used in assignments, read aloud, and even when they are placed on school library shelves. The main reason for this is the books' depictions of witchcraft, which, they argued, could contribute to delinquency. Misner then reveals that he finds this accusation difficult to believe, and if true, then argues that all Disney stories should be removed from schools as well. At this point in the passage, the author uses some humor, which though it is funny, distracts from the seriousness of the issue at hand. His sarcasm reveals that bias is prevalent in the issue, and as far as *Harry Potter* is concerned, he is a fan, and is willing to skew a supposed argument to prove his point. He does acknowledge the other side at least when he says, "I will not deny that the *Harry Potter* books contain violence" (Misner). However, after this acknowledgement, he begins to discuss Disney stories once more in a meaningless extended example. It does not connect with the rest of his arguments and seems a silly claim to make.

The end of this essay is summed up when he says, "Censorship restricts the growth of an individual, the advancement of knowledge, and the diversification of intellect. Censorship, contrary to those in favor of it rarely achieves its desired goal" (Misner). Though this may be what Jared Misner believes, his argument fails to allow readers to see every aspect of this claim that he makes. It fails to make the connections that are necessary.

The purpose of Misner's argument is a little unclear. Perhaps he is informing his readers of how censorship deprives American children of ideas and knowledge, or maybe he was simply promoting the *Harry Potter* series. His audience was probably a mix of American teenagers, as he was writing for a teen magazine, families with school age children, and school officials. Though the majority of his argument is solid and based upon fact, there are several instances that need major revision in order to be taken seriously.

Misner does do an excellent job, however, in conveying his strong opposition to censorship. He makes readers realize that schools removing quality, award winning literature and books for their students' safety and well being is both a sickening and mortifying activity. Books are one of society's main sources of knowledge that help shape and mold people's character. Books are responsible for helping to educate and further develop a person's love of reading. No school or government organization should be allowed to take that experience away from children. No matter the book, if it actively engages a child and makes him or her excited to read, then that book has made a difference and deserves a place of honor on a library shelf.

Work Cited

Misner, Jared. "The Silenced Sorcerer" *Teen Ink* 19.6 (Feb 2008): 34–34. *MAS Ultra School Edition*. EBSCOhost. 23 Sept. 2008 <http://web.ebscohost.com>.

Money, Money, Money, Money ...MONEY!

Kathryn Kremer

REMEMBER IN HIGH SCHOOL, when a good grade was worth nothing more than a "good job" and maybe a later curfew? The feeling of success that came with the approval was always worth the extra effort. Nothing else was needed to encourage students to try to succeed in school. In "Paying for Grades Devalues Education," Anthony Bradley effectively argues that paying students for good grades lessens students' character and lowers self motivation.

In this article, Anthony Bradley clearly states that he believes paying students for attaining a "good" grade is degrading. He gives several examples of school districts using this program and follows with examples of the damage that can be caused as a result of the program. Bradley also uses testimony from several professionals as to why this program is harmful, both to the student involved and their family. Bradley disputes the use of not only cash as a reward for grades, but also any other monetary incentives, such as cell phones. Clearly, he opposes the Sparks Incentive program and any other similar programs, believing students should work for their grades just for the knowledge they will gain.

Bradley presents a convincing argument with the use of an ethical appeal. The very first sentence of the article states that he is "a research fellow at the Acton Institute and assistant professor of Apologetics and Systematic Theology at Covenant Theological Seminary in St. Louis" (1). The Acton Institute regularly publishes academic books and articles in an effort to promote reduced government interventions in schools and businesses. Bradley frequently publishes articles concerning academics and is a well respected professor at Covenant Theological Seminary. Bradley also refers to a statement made by "clinical psychologist Dr. Madeline Levine" (1), a lecturer on child and adolescent issues. He is reinforcing his argument by using statements made by professionals respected in their fields of study. Bradley strengthens his argument by proving that he knows what he is talking about and that he consulted with professionals on the topic.

With the use of pathos, Bradley supports his argument that paying high school and elementary students for good grades is demeaning. He uses many distressing words in his article that would evoke any parent to believe that students should not be rewarded with money or any other gifts for achieving a good grade. He repeatedly uses phrases such as "deteriorate family relationships" (1), "misguided school" (1), "lessening of parental influence" (1), and "self centered materialism" (2). Any of these phrases would make a parent's heart stop and provoke them to think about what the effects of this program really are. No parent wants to lose their parental authority over their child, and they would like to believe that they can affect the outcome of their child's life. The harsh vocabulary usage in this article makes adults think about the results of a program that pays students for grades. Bradley repeatedly uses the phrase "bling bling" (1, 2), hinting that paying for grades promotes a mentality of easy money. Adults know that hard work pays off, and they don't want their child's future to be limited by the idea that money should always be at hand, that all they have to do is study.

Finally, Bradley appeals to logic to strengthen his case against paying for grades. He refers to a book, *The Price of Privilege*, written by Dr. Madeline Levine. He states that the book reveals "research shows that giving kids cash for grades is one of the most psychologically damaging approaches to education" (1). By saying this he is showing that rewarding grades with cash is known to harm a student's mentality about school. They will start looking at school as a way to make money, not to actually learn something that will help them get into college and make money in the future. He suggests that students will become all about right here and now, and not worry about what could happen to them in the near or distant future. Bradley promotes the belief that students who are paid for good grades will be more concerned with immediate gratification instead of the delayed rewards a good education can offer. Bradley also uses rhetorical questions to help readers understand that cash rewards degrade a child's character in the future, "Why is cultivating self centered materialism and breaking down parent/child relationships the only alternative to doing nothing?" (2). Paying for grades is not the only option to promote a child's want for education; students need to realize that education is a gift in itself, a promise of a better future. Teachers can help students to appreciate education by using different teaching methods and making the topics they cover more interesting to a teenage student.

This article is obviously intended for parents of children in high school. The language he uses clearly shows that he is appealing to adults to make a change in the school system. He continues to talk about "lessening parental influence" (1) and refers to failing family relationships and securities. This would make any parent anxious, even if they didn't have children attending a high school taking part in a program similar to the Sparks Incentive. No parent wishes to risk losing their child to material desires, nor do they want their children to grow into adults with "little humanity" (2). Bradley is trying to convince parents that this program is wrong and harmful to their children's future. He creates a compelling argument that few parents could argue with.

Bradley provides a strong argument against paying for grades. He uses pathos, ethos, and logos to clearly illustrate that the process is degrading and affects the student's future character and integrity. His belief is that education is not an immediate reward, but that students need to learn patience and wait for the future gratification of a good education. Students need to be self motivated to learn everything they can as a resource for future opportunities in life. In order to succeed, students need to know that not everything is easy and rewards are not always in the near future.

Works Cited

Bradley, Anthony. "Paying for Grades Devalues Education" *The Roanoke Times*. 24 August 2008. <http://www.roa noke.com/editorials/commentary/wb/174059>.

Wikipedia. *Acton Institute*. 21 August 2008. 28 September 2008. <http://en.wikipedia.org/wiki/Acton_Institute>.

Senator Barack Obama Successfully Addresses Race and Patriotism

Mandy Elliot

ON MARCH 18, 2008, Barack Obama delivered a speech that brought the highly controversial issue of race to the forefront of presidential debate. Obama, the Democratic presidential hopeful, decided to address the issue head on after footage of the sermon made by his former pastor, Reverend Jeremiah Wright, caused a huge uproar in the media. Reverend Wright had a habit of bringing his own radical views about the United States into his sermons. Video clips of his racial and anti American remarks caused many Americans to question their support for his church member, Barack Obama. Obama's speech begins by addressing the issue of these comments. He condemns the comments, but defends Reverend Wright as a person saying "As imperfect as he is, he is like family to me" (Obama 3). Next Obama when back into the past to explain some of the differences in black and white people today, such as education, income levels, etc. He explains how, working together, we can move past our differences towards a "more perfect union" (Obama 5).

In his speech, Obama had to address the entire nation, which included many different types of audiences. However, before he could do this, he had to establish a clear ethos for discussing a topics as controversial as race and patriotism. Obama did this successfully by revealing his "own American story" (Obama 1). He tells of how he, himself, is the product of an interracial marriage. This fact helps bridge the gap between racial lines in his audiences. He talks about his grandfather, who served his country in World War II, and his grandmother, who helped with war efforts at home by working on an assembly line. Both of these show he comes from a background of patriotism. Finally, he tells of how his wife "carries within her the blood of slaves and slave owners," connecting America's dark past of slavery with his life today. Obama states that while his story makes him a rather unconventional candidate for president, it is this background that has taught him that we, as Americans, are all one people, regardless of our differences (Obama 1). All of this sets up Obama's ethos very successfully. He was able to tie in nearly every audience type to his story, leaving everyone with a feeling of being connected. In response to an article written about Obama's speech in the Sun Times, one reader wrote that she was "behind Barack, his values and his keen, honest insight into America's past and future" (Sun Times).

The first audience Obama addresses is the one that is angry about the comments made by Reverend Jeremiah Wright. This is an important group because a majority of Americans seem to fall in this category. Obama connects with his audience by using pathos to tap into their emotions. He says "I have already condemned, in unequivocal terms, the statements of Reverend Wright that have caused such controversy" (Obama 2). He says that, like most people, he does not agree with everything that his pastor says. However, in regards to Wrights most recent comments, Obama says "the remarks . . .weren't simply controversial. . . . they expressed a profoundly distorted view of the country—a view that sees white racism as endemic, and that elevates what is wrong with America above all that we know is right with America" (Obama 2). Obama went on to defend Reverend Wright, pointing out that he was a good person and friend of Obama's. This was directed toward the audience who supported Reverend Wright regardless of his recent mistakes. Obama spoke of how Wright had been an inspiration to countless members of the church, including Obama, to embrace their faith and do good for one another. "As imperfect as he may be, he has been like family to me," Obama told us. (Obama 3).

Obama succeeded in convincing some readers he should not be held responsible for the actions of Wright. One such reader wrote, "I go to church and have been to many [of both] black and white [congregations] and I do not always agree with the message but I take what I need and leave the rest" (Sun Times). Many others, however, were not touched by his message of forgiveness toward Wright. They said Obama should not have stayed in a church where this kind of behavior was occurring. ". . . this man was Obama's mentor and someone he went to for advice." One reader responded. "Obama has to have the same beliefs or he would not have held this man in such high regard" (Sun Times).

Obama made use of pathos again as he quoted a portion of his book, Dreams From My Father, detailing the emotions he felt during his first service at Trinity. "People began to shout, to rise from their seats and clap and cry out, a forceful wind carrying the reverend's voice up into the rafters... and in that single note—hope!" (Obama 2). Yet even with this uplifting quotation, some readers found fault, saying Reverend Wright was influencing him, and so, his story should not be inspiring (Sun Times).

When Obama discussed how we should overcome the issue of race, he broke it into two audiences, the African American community and the white community. A few readers reacted badly to this form of separation saying "Obama is a racist" (Sun Times). To the African American community, Obama said "that path [towards unity] means embracing the burdens of our past without becoming victims of our past" (Obama 5) He pointed out using logos that African Americans should still demand what they deserve, but realize that people of other races, including white people, are demanding the same things, so we need to unite in those causes. One reader agreed with Obama saying "Why this obsession to keep reliving the past, unless those that believe ministers like the Reverend want to remain as victims" (Sun Times).

To the white community, Obama says we need to acknowledge that "what ails the African American people does not just exist in the minds of black people" (Obama 5). We need to admit that discrimination does still occur and help to work towards equality for all.

To the speech as a whole, there were many different reactions. Some believed Obama only addressed the race issue because he had to. Others said he used race to hide his shortcomings on other issues. One man said "[I] don't believe he has the ability to do the things he is talking about . . . I would love to have a 'Black' president (I am Black). But I much rather have an effective president black, white, male, female, or other" (Sun Times). However, overall, many people were touched and impressed by the speech. Obama was able to successfully address at least some members of every audience affected by this issue. One reader responded by saying "I have even more respect for the Senator that ever before" (Sun Times) They praised him for taking on this controversial issue with no fear. "Nobody that I can remember, has ever spoken in such an open, inclusive, and sensitive manner about race issues before," wrote Ted J. "I am proud to support this man for president." (Sun Times).

Works Cited

Obama, Barack. Transcript: Barack Obama's Speech on Race. *New York Times* March 18, 2008. Ocotber 2, 2008 <http://www.nytimes.com/2008/03/18/politics/18text obama.html>.

Obama's Addressing Race Issue Head on. Online Posting. March 18, 2008. *Sun Times*. <http://www.suntimes.com/news/commentary/847971,CST EDT edit18. article>.

Chapter Four:

Textual Responses

Malleable Minds: A Girl's Journey through Nature v. Nurture

Heather Bingham

ON A WARM SPRING AFTERNOON, as my friends prepared for finals on a vibrant college campus, I stood anxiously beside my father in the dim foyer of the old country church where he and my mother were married twenty years prior. The heavy wooden doors in front of us slowly opened, allowing the quickening sound of piano music to flood my ears. Donned in an elegant silk English style wedding gown, hand made by my grandmother, I breathlessly entered the stained glass glow of the sanctuary and surrendered my thoughts to the dizzying high of my fantasy wedding day. As a girl still emerging from the cocoon of childhood, motivated by the desire to follow in the footsteps of the previous young brides in my family, I joined my life to an easygoing preacher's son, who shared the same dream of settling into a country lifestyle and raising a family that I had treasured in my heart since childhood. As a naïve adolescent, enswathed in Christian family tradition and an isolated, country lifestyle, I could not have conceived of a different set of circumstances for my life. Everyone in my family has lived within ten miles of one another on the same land that the five original families of our relatives settled after sailing to the US from East Germany in 1838. The traditions of my family were as real to me as the visual images that I had learned from birth; green is to frog as red is to the clay soil of my native southern Ohio.

The world in which I found myself seven years later was shaped from a completely different mold than the world I perceived for myself on the outset of that hopeful spring afternoon. Unplanned events in the adult world I so envied as a girl have added a level of maturity to my thinking and enabled me to see how susceptible we humans are to our individual worlds and the experiences that occur as a result of our fabricated minds. We are not merely a homogenous species programmed to think and act a certain way; our lives and thoughts are individually shaped by innumerable, disparate factors. From the moment we take our first breath and open our eyes to the world around us, our minds begin to absorb the elements of our surroundings, developing ideas and cataloging memories, accumulating them over the period of a lifetime. Beginning with cherished childhood memories, a favorite toy or storybook, a best friend with whom secrets were shared in the glow of flashlights from under a make shift tent, and continuing into a concept of the type of person we desire to marry, our lives begin to reflect the phenotypic expression of our minds. While we are occupied with the task of day to day living, our minds undergo constant alteration from exposure to new information, individual interpretation, and acceptance of what we believe to be true in our own minds. Personalized knowledge emerges from a combination of perception by the natural senses and the congenital social learning to which we are inevitably exposed.

When I think of home, my mind formulates the image of a small, historic town surrounded by farm land, narrow rivers, and sparsely vegetated forests. The smoke stacks of a dark, occupation dictating paper factory rise grimly from the center of town, releasing a constant cloud of sulfuric fumes and black soot. Multiple generations of my family, along with the majority of men and women in my town, spend three hundred and sixty five days of their lives in the poorly ventilated factory, which constantly maims bodies and claims the lives of workers in its heartless, metal machines. It was not until I was removed from my family and the lifestyle of north eastern US and spent several years in the contradistinct lifestyle of the midwest that I discovered that the contoured concepts of my mind were, in fact, fluid, capable of acclimating new information and ideas about life. Scott Russell Sanders[1] speaks of a similar situation when he left behind the back roads of his boyhood home in Tennessee and Ohio to attend college. In Sander's[1] mind, the chief destinies for men were to become soldiers, "warriors," or physical laborers, "toilers." Men who labored with their bodies "got up before light, worked all day long whatever the weather, and when they came home at night they looked as though somebody had been whipping them."[1] The women he met in college carried in their minds a very different forged view of the men in their lives. Their fathers were successful men of power and privilege who served their towns as doctors, lawyers, bankers, architects; they ran the world. Because of his sex, these women viewed Sanders[1] as destined from birth to become like their fathers, and as a threat to their futures. For Sanders[1], who grew up in a town where the fate of men was as grim as the fate of women, the merging of these mentalities from contrasting worlds created, first bafflement, and then enlightenment. Sanders[1] and I likely drew comparable conclusions from our experiences: it is nearly impossible for the mind to escape from beyond the bounds of its carefully crafted idealogic analog without the introduction of new ideas and experiences. In the same way that I discovered that dirt could be brown as well as red, albeit full of rock in Missouri, I realized that there was a world beyond my world, brimming with diverse experiences and concepts to be discovered and absorbed into my mental archives.

One year after moving to Missouri, I lost the one safeguard and connection to home I had brought with me. In a dismal alteration of plans, my young husband and I decided to part ways in our discovery of a new life outside of Ohio. I was terrified of breaking away from the Christian principle that marriage is a permanent union, only to be ended in death, and become the first person in my family to dissolve a marriage. On the day of our annulment, I stood alone in the parking lot of the court house and watched my former husband somberly walk away from me, his head down, his hands in his pockets, downcast, personifying with his body the same emotions that were ripping through my heart. The image of the dark green suit I had never before seen him wear is burned into my memory. It was too small for him, probably obtained from the church's clothing donation bin, and it made him look more like a boy than a man. It was the kind of experience a perennial must undergo as its beautiful flower withers and dies and is used to fertilize a dormant seed in preparation for new growth in a future growing season. The process of recovering from such an experience encased my heart in a hard, protective covering, solidifying the mental transition from childhood into adulthood.

In the aftermath of such an emotionally exhausting journey, the most appropriate word I can use to describe my wedding day and my life with my new husband, Chris, is renaissance: rebirth. A second chance at love in marriage was a gift which provided me the opportunity to re evaluate the significance of words, actions, and the true relevance of a life long relationship with another person. My mind went through an unexpected transformation as I filtered out child like elements and allowed room for growth in a new phase of my life. I began to create an identity on the premise of my own ideas and desires rather than the philosophies of others, establishing a balance in the preservation of my life's history, while allowing room for change in my future. This novel process of discerning and defining my character in a second marriage was, for me, what leaving home to attend college is for most young adults. I utilized the opportunity to ponder and analyze the timeworn mentalities and traditions of my family and came to the same realization as Sanders[1], as one "who grew up in dirt poor farm country, in mining country... in the shadows of factories." Despite the alterations that occur to an individual's character through the unpredictable journeys of life, each person retains an identity, the ancient icon of previous family "toilers" and "warriors," that carry the undertow of a thousand generations.

As I increase in age and mature with time and exposure, I begin to understand that although I am a product of the events that comprised the early years of my life, my experiences and beliefs are not as absolute as they once seemed. When I was admitted to the state college in Missouri, an even greater plane of insight and information was exposed to me. As Mary Louise Pratt[2] suggests, "Despite whatever conflicts or systematic social differences might be in play, it is assumed that all participants are engaged in the same game and that the game is the same for all players." Rarely do individuals come from the same background and hold the same views of the world through their individual courses of learning. Realistically, there are likely no two people who have identical views on every position of knowledge. The world is far too diverse, experiences far too personal, and knowledge too readily available on vast planes of interpretation.

In an effort to better illustrate this concept, I refer to the documented observations of Horace Miner[3], a renowned anthropologist and professor of sociology and anthropology at the University of Michigan. Dr. Miner[3] conducted on going fieldwork among a poorly understood tribe of North American people known as the Nacirema. The Nacirema are geographically considered Americans, but as a result of their atypical magical beliefs, curious practices, and unusual behavior, their tribe name, *Nacirema*, was coined from a backward spelling of the word *American*. As with many secluded groups of individuals, the Nacirema have developed unique customs and beliefs, specific to their people, and upheld unquestionably by all tribe participants throughout the generations.

Not unlike many other North Americans, the Nacirema place a specific focus on the appearance and health of the body and have a fundamental belief that the human body is ugly, even detestable. Daily body rituals are carried out in every household. A "mouth rite" ritual is performed in secret and consists of inserting a small bundle of hog hairs into the mouth, along with magical powders, and performing a series of ritualized movements with the tongue. In addition to these mouth rite rituals, the people religiously seek out the services of a holy mouth man once or twice a year. Crude objects, such as hand fashioned augers, awls, and probes, are used in an "exorcism of the evils of the mouth in an almost unbelievable ritual torture of the client.[3] However barbaric and inconceivable these beliefs and practices may seem to an outsider, they are as steadfast and genuine to the Nacirema as the traditional Thanksgiving dinner is to many modern day Europeanized North American families.

Beliefs are nothing more than profound truths that have been adopted in one's own mind through recurring social exposure and culture. At different phases of life, most individuals come to the realization that the continued belief in a custom or tradition is a personal choice. It was several years after I chose to continue my belief in the Christmas magic of Santa Claus that I came to fully understand, accept and appreciate the more complex beliefs and heritage of my family. Similarly, individuals who participate in tribal rituals are making a conscious decision to do so. We allow our minds to adopt these beliefs as part of our system of knowledge, personally submitting to its further modification. The Nacirema are aware of the pain being inflicted on them and their children through the torturous practices of their tribe, but in an effort to avert physical and social decay, they mentally choose to endure the torture.

As humans living amidst a plethora of observable phenomenon, diversity, and ideals, it is universally ineludible that we each develop an individualistic anthology of accepted truths. We have no control over the origin of the journey and the elements to which we are initially exposed, yet as time elapses, decisions are made, pathways expand, and knowledge grows and evolves. The result is an extraordinary collage of unique individuals who exponentially enhance our world. From the back woods of conventional Ohio to remote tribes who hold conclusively to reconstructed societal ideals, the content of one's mind is the product of a distinct, individual world. We can be subconsciously molded by our individual worlds or consciously expose ourselves to a larger world in which we are able to make personal decisions that will direct the outcome of our identifications. The extent to which one is molded remains the control of the individual, and that is the beauty of the design.

References

1. Sanders SR. The Men We Carry in Our Minds. Compos
   ing knowledge: readings for college writers. Norgaard,
   R, editor. Boston, MA. Bedford/St. Martin's, 2007. pp.
   546–49.
2. Pratt ML. Arts of the Contact Zone. Composing knowl
   edge: readings for college writers.. Norgaard, R, editor.
   Boston, MA. Bedford/St. Martin's, 2007. p. 478.
3. Miner H. Body Ritual among the Nacirema. Compos
   ing knowledge: readings for college writers.. Norgaard,
   R, editor. Boston, MA. Bedford/St. Martin's, 2007. pp.
   340–43.

Princess Peach Shouldn't Have to Wear Pink

Bazil Manietta

A LONG TIME AGO, in a far away kingdom, lived a hero unrivaled in valor, renown, and ability. This otherwise ordinary man dedicated himself to the protection of the kingdom's royalty, often risking his very life to save the beloved princess of the land who was repeatedly victim to the plans of a dastardly infamous villain. No matter how hard she tried, the princess always seemed to fall into the clutches of this villain, helpless to escape without the help of the kingdom's courageous hero. This hero, known as none other than the world famous Mario, his princess, Peach, and the Mushroom Kingdom they live in represent a well known example of sexism and skewed gender roles in videogames.

This damsel in distress concept has been a part of videogame plots and game play from its beginning. In most cases, women in videogames are helpless victims, completely dependent on male protagonists to save them. Women are further degraded in videogames by often being represented as sexual objects, acting as little more than a physical prize for the protagonist, further gearing videogames toward men. Explosive action themes and gory guns fights also reinforce the male focus on videogames; even the language used in videogames is, more often than not, overwhelmingly more masculine than feminine, packed with superficial one liners and cheesy pick up lines used on the various damsels. It's obvious to most people that video gaming is something that is very male oriented. The way men and women are presented in videogames, the themes they are placed in, and how they are able to resolve problems is incredibly sexist. Men seem to always be in control, while women sit and look pretty, waiting for the protagonists rescue.

Since the days of Mario, women have had a lower status in videogames than men. In this classic 1980's adventure, the evil King Koopa kidnaps Princess Peach of the Mushroom Kingdom to keep her as his bride. Mario, a simple, Italian plumber, sets out to save the princess and in doing so must overcome Koopa's various goons. This is one of the earliest examples of underpowered women in video gaming. While Mario has a vast number of abilities with which he can fight off enemies, including the use of fireballs and flight, Peach apparently has no means of self defense. When Koopa attacks, all she is able to do is scream in peril and call desperately for Mario's help. Clad in her elegant pink dress and fragile high heels, Peach never shows signs of being anything but a victim.

This damsel in distress scenario was likely a social construction of the time. By the time of Mario's creation in the 1980's, women had already achieved much equality with men, though they were still often viewed as the subordinate gender during the birth of the videogame era. It seems natural, then, that Hollywood would also frequent the damsel in distress scenario. Videogames simply followed suit, proliferating the negative image to the younger gaming generation. As video gaming continued to grow, however, it didn't develop away from these female victim themes as much as movies did by placing women in powerful roles. Hollywood began to make films that went against the frail feminine image prevalent in the minds of most Americans by making women heroes and warriors. In the essay "The Men We Carry in Our Minds," Scott Russell Sanders uses his very first experiences in college after growing up in a poor family to illustrate the that people have clearly preconceived notions about gender deeply embedded in their minds, like the stereotypes of how men are powerful providers and women are domestic slaves (547). Those are the very stereotypes that Hollywood had begun to dissolve.

In cinema, producers and directors realized the importance of a female revolution. Sanders would likely say that movies like "Aliens" staring Sigourney Weaver and "Terminator" with Linda Hamilton strengthened the female persona by breaking the pre constructed social ideas of females that were prominent in our society. With videogames, though, little progress was made, even when women were cast as the protagonist, as with the Tomb Raider games. In the Tomb Raider series, Laura Croft is a pistol wielding, treasure seeking adventurer clad in shortie shorts and a belly button tank top; it only takes one glance at Ms. Croft's skin tight shirt and double D cup size to realize that her game isn't targeting women. Female sexuality is often exploited by the videogame industry in this way to appeal further to an already mostly male audience.

In the contrasting case of the game "Metroid Prime," which stars the female protagonist Samus, an attempt to positively fortify the female image fails unexpectedly. Throughout the game, the player knows Samus as a hero in a full body space suit, only discovering in the end that she is actually female. In this attempt to show that women can perform such a role just as well as a man through an unexpected twist, gender identity was completely lost and the experiment was unsuccessful. Samus is more frequently referred to as a robot or cyborg than a female human, especially by those new to the game. Many people find it easier to relate to Samus as a preprogrammed robot than break their idea of female frailty, an idea with which Sanders would likely agree. In her essay about the gender of slang and language, titled "Bitch," Beverly Gross cites the Freud in saying that the "male female nexus depicts male sexuality as requiring the admiration, submission, and subordination of the female" (508). Since Samus doesn't fulfill any of these requisites as an independent and strong woman, many male gamers tend to find it easier to ignore the fact that she's a woman, rather than believe that she is as capable as a man.

A recent game titled "Portal" is rather successful, however, at presenting a woman as a powerful, in control hero, albeit in a subtle fashion. The game centers on a prisoner in a mysterious scientific facility whose goal is to escape. The game is played entirely in the first person, meaning the player doesn't ordinarily have to opportunity to see the character being played. When starting the game, a vast majority of players assume that the protagonist is a man. There are a few instances during game play, however, in which the main character's reflection can be seen, making it very clear that the protagonist is, in fact, a woman. After this, it's very obvious that you're playing a digital woman who is performing just as a digital man would in the same scenario. The villain imprisoning you in the facility is also revealed to be female, and the only other character, an inanimate brick used to solve various puzzles, is even deemed to be "female." In fact, throughout the entire game, there isn't a single male character or voice; every character in the game is female (or at least possesses feminine traits, as in the case of the brick). No matter how initially subtle the female theme is, the game is plainly and successfully dominated by women in power.

Though it is the most obvious aspect of the game, the protagonist's gender isn't the only area where sexism exists in videogames. Action themes jam packed with explosions and car chases run rampant in videogame worlds. Situations men may find exciting, like a gun fight between Germans and Americans in a WWII setting, typically conflict with those that women find entertaining. In "Grand Theft Auto," the main character is (you guessed it) a man who does various jobs for a big city mob boss in a variety of violent manners. One highlight of the game is being able to pay a prostitute, receive a certain "service" in your car, and then immediately thereafter beat her to death with a baseball bat just to get your money back. This aspect of the game clearly targets men, as most women would likely be far more offended by this than men.

The language used by characters in various videogames also reflects a very male oriented industry. In the essay, "How Male and Female Students Use Language Differently," author Deborah Tannen explains how males and females differ in their lingual rituals. While women ritualize through personal exchanges and emotional connections, men "have their own, very different verbal ritual: a contest, a war of words in which they vie with each other to devise cleaver insults" (Tannen 498). As most protagonists are men, the language used by them reflects that, and characters interacting with the protagonist also tend to exhibit these same lingual patterns. In games such as "Team Fortress 2," where players compete against each other over the Internet, taunt actions are common in order to flaunt at the opposing team. Programmers and animators will often spend a great deal of time integrating mockery into a game. This is, of course, very appreciated by most male players, and perhaps considered annoying to many female players.

The majority of popular games developed today are made, primarily, by men and sold to men, with plenty of exceptions along the way. Even when women have a large amount to do in the development of videogame, however, it is still dominated by masculinity in order to appease the market. Development of the game "Assassin's Creed," for example, was lead by Ms. Jade Raymond, an accomplished videogame producer. Even though a woman spearheaded this project, the game was clearly sexist toward men, with the only prominent female character depending greatly on the male protagonist for support. Though this female character does greatly assist the protagonist along the way, there is never a point during which the male protagonist is entirely dependent on the supporting female character; the male protagonist is always in control and never loses it.

No matter what, it is likely that the Princess Peach will continue to be kidnapped by Koopa, and Mario will always be around to rescue her. It may be too late for Peach to recover her independence from Mario, but it certainly isn't too late for women to break into the videogame world as important and capable protagonists. The male and female image, themes, content, and language used in videogames are overwhelmingly sexist against women, though improvements and advancements toward a more balanced industry are taking place. With games like "Portal" focusing on strong, female protagonists, women gamers are beginning to find videogame role models with whom they can relate to and create idols out of as men commonly do. As gender equality continues to proliferate and technology becomes more prominent in our lives, videogames will likely begin to merge with the idea of male and female equity more. Women being portrayed as sexual objects will fade if consumers realize the blatant disrespect occurring in the industry and demand change. Mario would have probably been more insistent about a prenuptial agreement if he had foreseen the changes taking place in the rest of the videogame world.

Works Cited

Gross, Beverly. "Bitch." *Composing Knowledge*. Ed. Rolf
     Norgaard. Boston: Bedford/St.Martin's, 2007. 504–512.

Sanders, Scott Russel. "The Men We Carry in Our Minds."
     Composing Knowledge. Ed. Rolf Norgaard. Boston:
     Bedford/St. Martin's, 2007. 545–550.

Tannen, Deborah. "How Male and Female Students Use
     Language Differently." *Composing Knowledge*. Ed. Rolf
     Norgaard. Boston: Bedford/St. Martin's, 2007.
     496–501.

Wrestling with Anonymous Angels

Howard Simmons

THE FIRST AND ONLY TIME I convinced myself I had been "filled with the spirit," I had begun to develop a headache halfway through the experience. Kneeling at the altar, with a group of sweaty, passionate men grouped around me, I felt my tongue rolling inside my mouth. As desperate as a fish floundering upon dry land, it jumped back and forth, trying to form words which I was sure were coming soon. "You got it, brother," the pastor had ecstatically screamed. Soon my eyes had squirted the last tears, and still I held them shut – if I had opened them, the spell would be broken and all hope of speaking in tongues would be lost.

Eventually, I felt myself being carried away. The deacons and my father, finally broken by the late hour, had agreed among themselves that they would carry me to my car. I could sense an undercurrent of amusement had replaced their previous fervency.

As the car jostled down the road, I still kept my eyes shut. It wasn't until I arrived home and my mother greeted us at the door with the words, "He's faking," that I allowed myself out of that desperate trance. My fears and doubts were amplified by her cold gaze.

For several years I cowered through a sheltered life, lost in a haze of prayer meetings and Bible studies. I'd sit in a pew, sandwiched between my parents, and close my eyes, praying that I would be godly enough to earn salvation and overcome the sinful desires that always seemed to tempt me, if only in sordid fantasies.

At altar calls, I'd throw my head back, kneeling on well worn carpet, and pray again and again for God to fill me with

His Spirit. My tongue would wag and I'd bark nonsense, hopeful that what I was speaking was some hidden language that only God could understand and doggedly pushing the insistent doubts from my mind.

I'd whimper for some acknowledgment of His presence, of His forgiveness. But lying in bed on those nights, I'd become paralyzed by the sound of the refrigerator kicking on, so sure that it was actually Gabriel's trumpet sounding. All the saints had been called to be with God. Yet here I was, rigid between cotton sheets. During those times I realized I was utterly and completely alone and that my nature—my sinful nature, as the pastor spat before those altar calls—was something that was as much a part of me as my desire for the ability to overcome it. The feeling of solitude as I grew older became suffocating and I realized the One whom I was told was always there for me wasn't.

Left to find comfort alone, I pushed away from God and pulled anonymous angels toward me, tangling ourselves in the security of bed sheets as tightly as the rope securing the tongue tied protagonist in Robert Penn Warren's poem, "Arizona Midnight." The narrator, whom I picture as a grizzled old man, finds himself lost in his harsh surroundings. "The grief of the coyote," the "blunt agony" of a cactus, the quivering of the stars—all seem to have a place in that cold landscape. Yet the surveyor, able to identify the despair of that around him, is unable to give voice to his own sorrow, finding it instead through the unflinching world around him. He is acutely aware of life pushing forward despite grief and pain, but he is too overwhelmed by this very knowledge to follow its example. That poem, so obtuse in its meaning, echoes that hollow and unfathomable despair which ate holes inside me.

I feared that my needy fumblings in the seeming cloak of darkness were on display for the cold sky and whatever (or whomever) may be watching, like the young woman who finally succumbs to passion at the prompting of an unconcerned god in Donald Justice's poem of lost innocence, "In Bertram's Garden." In Justice's poem, a prim, innocent girl finds herself alone in a garden, disgraced and shamed after having been made dizzy by the bronzed Bertram, who has forgotten her in his sleep. The garden in which she hides offers no solace, and its impending decay of flowers and statues is a haunting picture of Jane's lost innocence and her sad future.

I, too, had given in to my sinful nature, and yet found no solace in those desperate wrestling matches. I often found myself awake after those nights of sweaty tangling, staring blindly at a ceiling which hid itself from me in darkness, suffocatingly close to my own bronzed boy, who, spent and exhausted, slept the peaceful sleep of the dead and naïve.

As lovers changed and the excuse of youth began to wear off, I found my desire for God, for love, had changed to a sharp, bitter, and all too painful ache that had somehow burrowed itself down into me further than any hope I'd felt at those altar calls as a child.

I could understand Langston Hughes's underlying current of anger and bitterness in his engaging and darkly funny essay "Salvation," a recounting of his salvation experience as a child at a revival at his aunt's church. At the special service "to bring the young lambs to the fold," Hughes found himself the last of two young men who had not felt the need to answer the altar call. The worshipers around him, unwilling to accept even the apathy of one soul, crowded him and through passionate pleas and a seemingly endless supply of painful patience, beckoned him to forgiveness. Their bullying desire to save his soul left him feeling guilty, not only for the fact that salvation never seemed to offer itself, but that he was unable to give them what they, and ultimately he, desperately wanted.

The revival congregants, who in their insistent fervency scared him more than the threat of damnation, were the same people with whom I shared a pew at my own church. Their intentions were good, but I could never completely succumb to their demanding hands which sought to impart God's will through contact with a sinner's flesh, or the earnest prayers which always left me hollow.

At the end of Hughes's essay, he is in bed, crying because Jesus never came to him. His relatives, meanwhile, mistake his tears for tears of repentance and joy, unaware that his salvation experience had resulted in exactly the opposite: having been let down by God, he had lost faith in Him.

For me, the loss of innocence, a gaining of knowledge, a search for God through the touch of His creation, led to the unmistakable truth that sometimes what we feel we need the most and for which we search the most desperately cannot be found.

Works Cited

Hughes, Langston. "Salvation." *The Big Sea: An Autobiog raphy*. NY: Hill & Wang, 1993. 18–20.

Justice, Donald. "In Bertram's Garden" *New and Selected Poems*. NY: Knopf, 1997. 49.

Warren, Robert P. "Arizona Midnight." *The Collected Poems of Robert Penn Warren*. Baton Rouge, LA: Louisiana State UP, 1998. 536.

Appendix

English 110 Course Description and Goals

Course Description:
• Critical reading and writing skills applicable to writing within and beyond the college community. Emphasis on composition processes, argumentation of diverse issues, and collaborative learning, such as peer review.

Course Goals:
1. Develop a rhetorical understanding of writing, including how purpose, audience, the rhetorical situation, voice, tone, and genre conventions affect writing choices.

2. Develop a fuller understanding of the student's own writing process, practicing a range of strategies for composing, drafting, and revision.

3. Develop critical reading and writing skills, including writing as a mode of learning and active reading, where scholarly annotation and written reading responses amplify the reading process. Students will also learn to synthesize sourced material with their own argument and understand how the concepts of audience and authority interact with this process.

4. Develop knowledge of writing conventions, including common forms of academic writing. Students will practice appropriate means of documenting their research using a style such as MLA, and also control surface features such as syntax, punctuation, and spelling.

5. Increase the unity, coherence, cohesiveness, and clarity of student writing through editing for effectiveness in global and

paragraph organization, sentence structure, word choice, and style. Students will also learn the difference between editing and revision by utilizing both processes in their writing.

6. Understand the ethics of academic writing, which includes avoiding racist, sexist, or otherwise derogatory language. Students will also learn the norms of academic honesty and the consequences of plagiarism.

7. Develop skills in conducting and evaluating research in order to support and inform their own writing. Students will practice using resources such as libraries, research databases, and the Internet. They will also familiarize themselves with the conventions of *MLA* documentation.

Standard Classroom Policies for the Composition Program at Missouri State University

Academic Dishonesty:

Missouri State University is a community of scholars committed to developing educated persons who accept the responsibility to practice personal and academic integrity. You are responsible for knowing and following the university's student honor code, *Student Academic Integrity Policies and Procedures*, available at www.missouristate.edu/ assets/provost/AcademicIntegrityPolicyRev 1 08.pdf   and also available at the Reserves Desk in Meyer Library.

Addendum: The Composition Program does not allow the use of "double duty" papers (a single paper turned in to two or more classes). Student writing must be original to the composition course it is turned in for. "Double duty" papers will be considered cheating.

Statement of Disability Accommodation:

To request academic accommodations for a disability, contact the Director of Disability Services, Plaster Student Union, Suite 405, (417) 836–4192 or (417) 836–6792 (TTY), www.missouristate.edu/disability. Students are required to provide documentation of disability to Disability Services prior to receiving accommodations. Disability Services refers some types of accommodation requests to the Learning Diagnostic Clinic, which also provides diagnostic testing for learning and psychological disabilities. For information about testing, contact the Director of the Learning Diagnostic Clinic, (417) 836–4787, http://psychology.missouristate.edu/ ldc.

Statement of Non Discrimination:

Missouri State University is an equal opportunity/ affirmative action institution, and maintains a grievance procedure available to any person who believes he or she has been discriminated against. At all times, it is your right to address inquiries or concerns about possible discrimination to the Office for Equity and Diversity, Park Central Office Building, 117 Park Central Square, Suite 111, (417) 836–4252. Other types of concerns (i.e., concerns of an academic nature) should be discussed directly with your instructor and can also be brought to the attention of your instructor's Department Head. Please visit the OED website at www. missouristate.edu/equity/.

Dropping a Class:

It is your responsibility to understand the University's procedure for dropping a class. If you stop attending this class but do not follow proper procedure for dropping the class, you will receive a failing grade and will also be financially obligated to pay for the class. For information about dropping a class or withdrawing from the university, contact the Office of the Registrar at 836–5520.

Classroom Etiquette:

The course instructor has original jurisdiction over his/ her class and may deny a student who is unduly disruptive the right to attend the class. Students are expected to master the course content in compliance with the syllabus of the course instructor. The student is expected to comply with all reasonable directives of the course instructor. The course instructor may have a student administratively withdrawn from a course upon showing of good cause and with the concurrence of the department head. The appeals process in case of such administrative withdrawal shall be as stated in the academic regulations under "Grade Re evaluation Based on Performance."

Cell Phone Policy:

As a member of the learning community, each student has a responsibility to other students who are members of the community. When cell phones or pagers ring and students respond in class or leave class to respond, it disrupts the class. Therefore, the Office of the Provost prohibits the use by students of cell phones, pagers, PDAs, or similar communication devices during scheduled classes. All such devices must be turned off or put in a silent (vibrate) mode and ordinarily should not be taken out during class. Given the fact that these same communication devices are an integral part of the University's emergency notification system, an exception to this policy would occur when numerous devices activate simultaneously. When this occurs, students may consult their devices to determine if a university emergency exists. If that is not the case, the devices should be immediately returned to silent mode and put away. Other exceptions to this policy may be granted at the discretion of the instructor.

Moon City Press is a joint venture of the Missouri State University
Departments of English and Art and Design.
With series lists in "Arts and Letters" and
"Ozarks History and Culture,"
Moon City Press
features collaborations
between students and faculty
over the various aspects of publication:
research, writing, editing, layout and design.

Printed by Missouri State University Printing Services.